In loco parentis:
A Teacher's Guide to
Educational Administration

V.K. GILBERT

A.T. SHEEHAN

K.G. TEETER

Guidance Centre
Faculty of Education
University of Toronto

Canadian Cataloguing in Publication Data

Gilbert, V.K. (Vernon Keith), 1927–
    In loco parentis : a teacher's guide to
educational administration

ISBN 0-7713-0204-5 √

1. School management and organization.
2. Teacher participation in administration.
3. Teacher-student relationships. I. Sheehan,
A.T. II. Teeter, K.G. (Kenneth G.), 1927–
III. University of Toronto. Faculty of Education. Guidance Centre. IV. Title.

LB2805.G54 1985   371.1   C85-098604-4

Contents

1   The Role of Theory and Research in Administration

1 The Role of Theory and Research in Administration

Many teachers and student teachers question their involvement in the administration of schools. Administration, to them, is something that happens in the front office; they do not seem to realize that they also play an important part in the every-day functioning of the school. Many also question the place of theory and research in education, often dismissing them as impractical or little use in the classroom.

It is the intention of the authors to point to the relationship between the practical and the theoretical. The authors believe that all teachers have an administrative role to play, ranging from the humblest act of sending someone for more chalk, to the negotiating in a staff meeting about which textbooks should be used.

"Administration" has many meanings. As a discipline, it is taught in different guises—business administration, public administration and more recently, educational administration. The same principles underlie each but are manifested differently.

Educational administration as a study in its own right dates from the end of World War II. Prior to this, the study of administration most often consisted of an overview of school law, and political and financial factors. The lessons were delivered by those who had fought the good fight in the trenches; the military metaphor was appropriate. In 1950, in the United States the Cooperative Program in Educational Administration was begun. It was financed by the Kellogg Foundation and sponsored by three groups of educational officials. This project—designed to improve educational administration—triggered a vast increase in activities. Research expanded as more money was put into projects; indeed, so much was being done that educational administration, for a time, moved to the forefront as it developed new concepts in administration and leadership.

Similar studies inevitably followed in Canada and elsewhere. In 1952, the Canadian Education Association (CEA) secured funding from the Kellogg Foundation for a project in educational leadership. It ran until 1956 and had the support of many provincial ministries of education and prominent educators. Various journals also began dealing with administration, although for a time research and writing focussed on the mechanical side: timetabling, bus routes, planning buildings. Inevitably, in the 1960's, the study of administration turned to three major topics: the dichotomous study of interrelationships of organizations and people; the bureaucracies of schools; and the quantifying of leadership and organization, through two well-known and widely-used instruments, the Leader Behavior Description Questionnaire (LBDQ) and the Organizational Climate Description Questionnaire (OCDQ).

More recently, associations of administrators have sprung up. In Ontario, for example, the Ontario Council for Leadership in Educational Administration developed the conceptual side, using workshops, papers, and publications. Through graduate courses at the Ontario Institute for Studies in Education (OISE), hundreds of teachers have studied the theory that underpins the practice of administration.

The number of associations has increased in recent years; on the practical side, provincial organizations, like the Ontario Association of Education Administrative Officials (OAEAO), have brought administrators together to discuss their problems; at the national level, the Canadian Association for the Study of Educational Administration (CASEA) serves both administrators and professors of educational administration. As a member group in the Canadian Society for the Study of Education (CSSE), CASEA provided a forum for its members through publications at the meetings of CSSE during the annual conferences of the Learned Societies.

Thom (1979) presents an authoritative picture of the situation in Canada, including personnel, trends, publications, and a directory of courses. It is an impressive list, all the more because most developments have occurred within the past twenty years. No doubt the founding of OISE in 1965 has had much to do with the progress, for the institute teaches graduate courses in education to thousands of teachers and attracts scholars, both as faculty and students, from all over the world. The Ontario Ministry of Education has helped through its research funds and by demanding credits in graduate courses as part of the requirements for the principals' and supervisory officers' qualifications. Despite the economic problems of the 1980's, the future for educational administration still manages to look bright.

1.1   The Place of Theory

A common reaction to ideas about education is, "Oh, that's all right in theory, but it won't work in practice." Frequently, the use of the term "in theory" is a mistake: what is meant is "ideally." Indeed, a good theory is the underpinning of practice; an aircraft designer, for example, would be extremely foolish to disregard the laws of gravity when designing an aircraft. Far from representing an abstract "ideal," theory represents a systematic attempt to explain observations made in practice. Although values are not part of theory, theory often sets standards for administrators and teachers. Halpin (1958) discusses this misconception, this confusion between "real" and "ideal." Simon (1957) writes that, although administrators and teachers need standards, these standards, which are values, are not theory as defined above. We need only look at the exhortations for teachers and pupils in the Acts and regulations to see such examples as "It is the duty of a teacher to teach diligently..." and "it is the duty of a pupil to submit to such discipline as would be exercised by a kind, firm and judicious parent..." All very well "in theory," but how can one always be a kind, firm, and judicious parent? It is more important, from a theoretical point of view, to explain why one cannot attain the ideal and to present some framework for the views expressed in standards. Griffiths (1959) writes that we can understand what theory is by emphasizing what it is not; it is not abstract speculation, or a philosophy, with its attendant values, or a personal approach to doing the job, or a synonym for "impractical."

A theory consists of assumptions, definitions, hypotheses and concepts; these are connected in a systematic way for making predictions and explaining observed phenomena. In schools and school systems, the phenomena include the behaviour of the people in the organizations and the relations between them.

It should be emphasized again that sound theory is built on observation of facts—not always an easy task in the social sciences. Measurement, for example, creates many difficulties in the selection and validation of instruments. In the social sciences, facts are not as clear-cut as in the physical sciences; "they-me" phenomena may well be interpreted differently by different observers. Indeed, the presence of an observer in an organization can influence behaviour, no matter how aloof that observer tries to be. And the gathering of data in the social sciences, unlike the physical sciences, is still relatively undeveloped. From the data, the social scientist develops concepts to put the mass of factual material into some order. The concepts then can be related one to another to form a framework from which further ideas may be developed for hypotheses. Hypotheses test the tentative "theory" or framework. Either they confirm it, little by little, or else they contradict it. Paradoxically, the contradictions can sometimes lead to modifications that reconfirm the theory. If a theory is widely tested and universally accepted, it may be called a "law," but even laws are subject to modification, as we see with respect to Einstein's work and Newton's law of gravity.

It is important, however, for teachers to realize that education, especially its administration, has its facts, concepts, theories, and hypotheses. Blindly following myths and "what everyone knows" is not always best. Common sense, after all, is what tells us that the earth is flat.

The classroom teacher can assist the research in education by keeping an open mind about traditional practices, by co-operating with researchers, by systematically recording observations, looking for patterns, and by reading the literature and keeping informed. Educational administration has come a long way in twenty years, but it still needs much investigation. The increasing assumption of power by teachers is one area where some systematic explanation of administration could prevent many confrontations and conflicts among teachers, administrators, and trustees.

Figure 1.1

			hypotheses
	hypotheses	conflict	
confirm		modify	
	theory		theory
concept	concept	concept	
	assumption definition		
observation	observation	observation	

2   Organizational Theory

2 Organizational Theory

2.1 Organizations Defined and Described

The analysis of organizations has progressed beyond finding solutions to problems encountered by those in authority. It has expanded and then spawned other disciplines in an attempt to understand the concept of "organization." Organizational analysis has gone far afield, from the concentration on the formal structure by the disciples of scientific management, to the almost exclusive interest in social relationships that followed the Hawthorne Studies.

Defining an "organization" is difficult; the common elements are groupings, people, specific goals, a deliberate element of establishment, and a set of rules. Parsons (1960) defines the organization as a social unit, constructed to seek specific goals. Blau and Scott (1963) add to Parsons' list "rules and a formal status structure, with clearly marked lines of communication and authority." To distinguish between organizations as defined above (businesses, armies, churches) and those social groupings (friends, families) with a loose structure of control but no framework of formal goals, the term "social organization" is applied to the latter.

Labels are all very well, but caution is necessary when examining the characteristics of organizations. Typologies help in understanding organizational structure to some degree, although they may not explain the relationships within.

In his typology by goals, Parsons (1960) distinguishes four types according to their contributions to society:

- Production — the creation of consumer goods
- Political — the control and distribution of power in society
- Integrative — the securing of co-operation in society, the settling of conflicts

— Pattern maintenance—the provision of continuity through educational and cultural activities.

Many organizations straddle more than one category as they engage in different activities. When we examine a school in terms of Parsons' types, at first glance it falls into the fourth type. Upon reflection, however, we see perhaps that a school is also engaged in controlling power in society; many critics of the educational system claim that the present structure seeks to perpetuate the status quo economically and politically. The prime value of categorizing organizations seems to be in the raising and consideration of such questions.

Going beyond the function of organizations, Katz and Kahn (1966) proposed a list of basic characteristics, expressed in each case in the form of a continuum:

— Organizations that transform people vs. those that transform objects
— Those with rewards intrinsic to the operations vs. those that enable satisfaction to be sought extrinsically
— Structure of the organization, closed vs. open, including hierarchical structure and the distribution of rewards to members
— Degree of use of resources, equilibrium vs. growth

Placing a school or a school system on Katz and Kahn's model raises some questions. How open is the school towards people? How intrinsic or extrinsic are the rewards, and do they differ? Why? All are fascinating topics for a professional development day.

Etzioni (1964) used the concept of control as a basis for classification. He describes control as the manner in which participants in an organization relate to the authority system. His categories of control are:

— Coercive—the use of physical means of control
— Utilitarian—the use of material means for control purposes
— Normative or persuasive—the use of appeals to group norms or symbols

Etzioni explains how different forms of power lead to different consequences. Generally speaking, coercive power is of course the most alienating to those subjected to it, and normative is the least. Control varies according to rank; those toward the bottom of the hierarchy are subject more often to coercive control, those at the top to persuasive or normative. This hierarchy appears to be the norm in the schools. In recent years, however, control over pupils has shifted from the coercive towards the normative. The objectives may well be the same, but the strategies of change have altered to a remarkable degree in twenty years. Consultation, appeals, persuasion, and a search for understanding now take up much of a teacher's or a principal's time.

Blau and Scott (1963) developed a typology based upon the "prime beneficiary" of the organization. The classifications are as follows:
- Mutual benefit associations, in which the membership benefits
- Business firms, the owners
- Service organizations, the clients
- Commonweal organizations, the public at large.

In this model, the school is primarily a service organization, but is also commonweal to some extent. Considering schools in this fashion leads to the question, who is the client group? Parents, pupils, and the public all have claims; one of the difficult tasks confronting principals, supervisory officers, school boards, and the ministry of education itself, is the balancing of different interest groups. And with the addition of the conflict between professional and public control, there is a good possibility conflict will easily arise. Conflict is not necessarily destructive; the search for a solution can lead to quite unexpected and constructive acts.

From this general discussion of the nature of organizations, we shall go on to examine some of the main threads in the development of organizational analysis. Amongst them, two in particular—scientific management and human relations—have had a significant influence on schools. After that discussion, we shall look at others that have also profoundly affected educational systems—bureaucracy and professionalism.

2.2   Classical Management Theory

Scientific management grew from the work of F. W. Taylor, who applied engineering skills and scientific knowledge to the study of work and of workers. Taylor became an engineer in an iron works and began to put into practice some of the principles of efficiency he had developed during his college days. At that time, he had directed his energies to the sporting field, but now he was able to develop his principles in his work. He applied his methods to the output of workers, a radical idea at the time; although managers could be expected to know how much a machine could produce, no one had systematically studied the output of workers. If it proved possible to estimate how much a certain worker could produce, then it would be possible to formalize the findings and use them as a standard by which to measure other employees' capacities. The next logical step would be to improve the efficiency of each worker by determining the best possible way of performing a given task.

Taylor faced much opposition in his attempts to introduce his new system. Those who obviously stood to benefit were enthusiastic, but the unions, which feared that increased efficiency would mean loss of employment, were opposed. It had already happened that workers on piece-work had to produce more for the same amount of pay, once management had discovered how much more the workers were capable of.

Taylor tried to distinguish between the principles of his approach and the methods by which this system was put into practice. He blamed two sources: "first, faulty management; and second, soldiering on the part of the workers" (Callahan, 1962). He believed that managers were to blame because they did not apply the principles correctly.

Taylor maintained there was one best way to do a job, which could be found by experiments; once determined, this method should be applied rigorously. Many managers, however, were content to let workers do routine tasks by methods handed down over the years, whether or not they were the most efficient. His second cause was with the workers; their "soldiering", he believed, was of two types: "natural" (laziness) and "systematic." The natural laziness, he contended, was regrettable, but could be handled by pressure from management, if applied expertly. It was the systematic "soldiering" that was more difficult to deal with. (Even now, it does not appear to have left us; we still hear of "feather-bedding" and "fiddling.") Taylor disagreed that more efficient work would cause loss of jobs, or less pay, or more work for the same pay. He believed that decreased prices meant that more goods would be bought, thereby improving the standards of living. It was difficult to induce workers and management to accept his principles of scientific management.

Taylor believed that his system was better even than incentive and bonus schemes because it also depended upon sound principles of management. In his book *The Principles of Scientific Management*, he enunciated his four principles:
- The old traditional rule-of-thumb method for doing a job is to be replaced by a method based upon a scientific evaluation of the task.
- A deliberate element of choice of worker for the job is to be introduced, together with specific job-training.
- Management sets goals and supervises; workers carry out the tasks set for them.
- Management assumes responsibility for setting objectives, a task to which it is better suited. Co-operation in determining the roles of management and workers is established.

From the workers' point of view, these principles meant that they were to do exactly as instructed, with no argument, and to show no initiative; management determined all actions. If the workers did as instructed, they were rewarded with increased pay. In time, however, they came to resent the presence of the time and motion study experts; many considered it a form of exploitation, designed only to increase profits for the company. Indeed, this was Taylor's view of the purpose of a business. He did not hesitate to lay off workers if his methods showed they were no longer required. To some extent, his success depended on the number of redundancies.

The efficiency movement nevertheless had a lasting impact on schools and the organization of school systems. Many school inspectors not only observed teachers teaching, but also commented on the height of the blinds and the number of lights left on after a class had been dismissed. Callahan (1962) reports that in the United States in the early part of the century, superintendents emphasized efficiency and detailed, uniform, work procedures. One would like to think that Canadian schools escaped this trend—for the evidence one way or the other is scanty—but the public school inspector certainly had much influence, and many boards of education saw it as one of their prime duties to keep the mill rate down. Although they pre-dated Taylor, the rigid curricular and text-book lists of the past included some of the spirit of scientific management.

The fragmentation of tasks into small steps, each easily supervised, has a strong appeal, at least from the supervisor's point of view. Discipline in the classroom carries the same strain in its background; children in rows, sitting still, moving only when told, all have as their objective a clean, tidy, efficient school.

In these tough economic times, scientific managers of the 1980's use similar methods to bring workers into line; these latter-day Taylors take quite seriously their responsibilities to set objectives. They can also be found in the ministries of education. The universities in Ontario, for example, face close scrutiny in budgetary matters; under certain circumstances they can come under the control of a government-appointed manager. A special commission into university affairs recently recommended drastic measures to rationalize programs.

One significant change is occurring, however, in the politics of education. In schools, at least, the teachers' federations are becoming much more militant and are demanding—and frequently getting—a greater say in their working conditions. Although this trend takes away some of the authority of the school principal, it is increasing the collegiality of the school staff. Those provinces that gave the teachers the right to strike also granted them more say in running the schools.

Taylor was not the only person working on principles of management. Concurrently, two men, both of whom greatly influenced management and organizational structure, were developing their own themes. Max

Weber, a German sociologist, designed his ideal bureaucracy as a tool to overcome many of the shortcomings he saw in nineteenth-century organizations. (We shall deal with Weber and his concept later in this chapter, under a separate heading.)

The second person of note was Henri Fayol, who developed a list of principles designed for good management. Whereas Taylor had been interested primarily in the production line and the efficiency of workers, Fayol's schema was directed towards managers themselves. Fayol's list was in the same spirit as Taylor's, a list to be followed, but not accompanied by any attempt to conceptualize or to work towards a theory of organizations. Although scientific management has largely been superseded, it is worth noting Fayol's list because so many of the elements were adapted to school management. The list contains over a dozen items, but we shall mention only some of the more important.

Division of work is necessary. Jobs should be broken into small tasks so that workers need work on only a few. Secondary schools practise this, but elementary schools are beginning to lean towards greater specialization. For example, they have grade chairmen, division chairmen; and "special education" has many specialized fields.

Authority must be clearly established so that all know who is in charge of whom or what. Most boards and principals issue lists and charts which include positions, duties and who is responsible to whom. Many schools issue a teacher's handbook with similar information.

A clearly delineated line of command is desirable. Each person should have only one boss to whom to report and from whom to receive instructions. Fayol's principles are held in most schools. Even attempts to change them through the introduction of team teaching, group work, open-plan classrooms and the like, have met with only limited success, mainly in elementary schools.

Renumeration should be fair, but should also be impersonal and subject to rules. A standard grid is far preferable to any scheme of merit pay or rating. In general, teachers' federations have steadfastly opposed the few sporadic attempts to introduce merit pay. In universities, merit ratings seem to lead to a quantification of efforts, so that no one is certain what merit is; after a while, it often degenerates into a reward for creative writing.

Decision-making should be centralized. Such a policy ensures complete co-ordination from the top down. Schools follow this principle in varying degrees; much depends upon the principal's attitude towards the professional status of the teacher. We will argue for increased professionality and more responsibility for principals and teachers. Apparently at the level of the board of education office, Fayol is alive and well, for board buildings increase in size, to some extent to accommodate the increasing numbers of supervisory officers carrying out centralized decision-making. The argument will no doubt continue; one of the unsolved puzzles in public education is the problem of the professional working within a public system.

Comments along the same lines could be made for the remaining items in the list. For those seeking positions with boards, some of the items could well make good questions to pose for the interviewers, to help the applicant decide what kind of management exists within the school or system.

A third writer who has had a significant impact upon schools is Luther Gulick. He was responsible for the acronym POSDCORB developed in his study of the U.S. presidency. By analysing what presidents actually did, he established his list: planning, organizing, staffing, directing, coordinating, reporting and budgeting (Gulick and Urwick, 1931). This list, together with Gulick and Urwick's emphasis on charts of responsibility and lists of duties, had a noticeable effect upon schools. The charts and lists are still popular; it is highly likely that each teacher's manual contains several. They certainly help in sorting out who does what to whom and with what, at least in a formal sense. But what they do not tell us is who is responsible to have this done, or to influence a decision, or to block a proposed change. For example, the Grade V budget clerk at the board office seldom appears in such a chart, yet this person makes many decisions affecting the daily life of the school: the timetable expert also seldom appears on an organizational chart, yet is in charge of one of the most important tools of decision-making in the school.

2.3   Human Relations: A Concern for People

Not only workers and unions, but also writers in industrial psychology, began to react against the scientific management approach. Among them was Mary Parker Follett (1868-1933), who wrote a series of papers arguing that people in organizations should work together harmoniously and that it was management's task to build such a relationship.

Follett and others believed that it took more than pleasant physical surroundings to make workers contented.

Follett was in the vanguard of the movement away from the strictly formal and authoritarian model of management, but it was not from her that the major impetus came when finally a change of approach arrived.

It is widely considered that the experiments of Elton Mayo and Fritz Roethlisberger at the Hawthorne Plant of the Western Electric Company in Cicero, Illinois (conducted around 1927 to 1932) were the kingpin in the development of the human relations approach. Mayo and Roethlisberger, however, were not in any way setting out to establish a human relations approach when they began their experiments. They were industrial psychologists commissioned to test the effects of lighting in the plant. This approach was quite normal for the times, for industrial psychologists frequently tested against production such variables as temperature, lighting, rest pauses, and noise. And how did work mates affect production? As Brown (1954) asked: if four men can each shovel 25 tons of material a day, can four men working together be expected routinely to shovel 100 tons per day?

The earliest experiments at the Hawthorne Plant studied the effects of lighting levels, rest periods and length of the work day upon production (Roethlisberger and Dickson, 1939). Three experiments were performed to study the effects of change in illumination. When lighting was increased and decreased, production changes did not correspond in any identifiable pattern. More tests were conducted, involving control groups and test groups; in both cases, production efficiency increased. Obviously something more than changes in illumination affected production. Because it had already been found that social groups formed in industrial plants on the shop floor and that these same groups determined workers' behaviour to some extent, the company commissioned Mayo and Roethlisberger to design further research into group structure and behaviour.

Mayo and Roethlisberger chose the bank-wiring room, one department where the effect of pay incentives on group activities had been strong. Suspecting that they were looking for something that went on between the workers (that is, the personal relations and their ways of performing the job), the researchers decided against setting up an experiment to measure efficiency. Instead, they posed six questions:

- Do workers really become tired?
- Are rest pauses desirable?
- Is a shorter working day desirable?
- What are the attitudes of workers towards their work and their company?

- What is the effect of changing equipment?
- Why does production drop in the afternoon?

(Brown, 1954)

These are obviously psychological questions.

The bank-wiring room employed fourteen men to connect wires to pieces of telephone equipment; nine actually attached the wires, three soldered them, and two acted as inspectors. In order to preserve the *status quo ante* as far as efficiency was concerned, the research was carried out carefully so that behaviour would be observed, and production norms would not be changed. One of the two in the team acted as a non-participant observer, merely noting what went on in the room without being at all committed; in fact, he seemed to be quite disinterested. The other member never entered the room; in complete confidentiality, he interviewed workers about the job, their feelings towards it, their own personal values and habits.

The study found that, within the group, the men had managed to produce their own pecking order (Ownes, 1981). But, those to whom the group granted authority were not always those whom management had placed there. The group decided how much production would be achieved, regardless of any incentives schemes offered by management; indeed, they appeared indifferent to them. (Witness here, also, teachers' reactions to merit pay and other changes in methods of payment.) Brown (1954) notes that the unofficial code of behaviour that emerged had a strong influence over the members. It was built around the following rules:

- You should not turn out too much work. If you do, you are a "rate-buster."
- You should not turn out too little work. If you do, you are a "chiseller."
- You should not tell a supervisor anything that will be a detriment of an associate. If you do, you are a "squealer."
- You should not attempt to maintain social distance or "act officious." If you are an inspector, for example, you should not behave like one.

Brown (1954) advises the following:

Firstly, that no collection of people can be in contact for any length of time without such informal groupings arising and natural leaders being pushed to the top. Secondly, that it is not only foolish but futile to try to break up these groups; a wise policy would see to it that the interests of management and workers coincided to such an extent that the collection of informal groups which makes up a factory would be working towards the same goals instead of frustrating each other's efforts.

This then was the basis of the human relations approach that emphasized human factors in ordering the daily affairs of the organization. From this, many new concepts developed, all useful tools for management. These included morale, "democratic" supervision, group dynamics, and involvement of workers in affairs of the organization. Eventually, these ideas began to filter into schools and school systems; in some, but by no means all cases, they began to replace the authoritarian images of the superintendent, inspector and principal, long held and reinforced by the principles of scientific management. There were further repercussions for the bureaucratic model, which had much in common with the scientific management approach.

Two themes run through studies on management and leadership. On the one hand, they do not emphasize efficiency, getting the job done; on the other hand, they are concerned about the human side of the operation and the dynamics of the work group. Both themes made a great impact upon schools and school systems. They emerge in various guises throughout the literature.

2.4   Bureaucracy

The popular notion of "bureaucracy" is some kind of woolly organization bound up in "red tape," in which nothing is ever done on time, if it is ever completed at all. The word "bureaucratic" has become a synonym for slow, inefficient ways of doing things. But the ideal bureaucracy, as defined by Max Weber, is designed to be anything but slow and inefficient. Indeed, he proposed it as an organizational structure to achieve goals in an efficient manner. In this regard at least, it has a kinship with scientific management.

Only a few large complex organizations, the church and armies, for example, existed before the industrial revolution. Hierarchical in nature, they had some elements of Weber's bureaucracy, but were also subject to other forms of control. Studying the possible impact of these changes upon society, he examined contemporary organizations. Of the various structures he studied, he favoured the bureaucratic type, for it presented itself as "rational and unbiased, and avoided the use of human emotion and favoritism in the making of administrative decisions" (Owens, 1970).

Weber identified three forms of organization: the "charismatic" organizations, in which a single leader commanded loyalty by his mere presence (the Pied Piper syndrome); the "traditional" organizations, in which managerial positions were handed down either through families or through some kind of "old-boy" network; and the "bureaucratic" organizations, in which offices (bureaus) were filled by those best able to do the job.

Weber refined the bureaucratic-style of organization into what he designated the "ideal-type bureaucracy". This was based upon the use of technical expertise, intended to function efficiently but at the same time sharing characteristics with other organizational structures. He proposed to use rationality as the basis of administration, by emphasizing the role rather than the person who filled it, and by ordering these roles so that the work of the organization was done in an efficient manner. The characteristics of his organizational structure are as follows:
  — Specialization through division of labor and responsibility
  — Hierarchy of authority
  — Consistent system of written rules and regulations and policies
  — Impersonal orientation in relationships
  — Development of long-term careers in the organization, based on competence.

The five characteristics were intended to promote efficiency in decision-making, in performance of tasks and in achieving goals. In these respects, the bureaucracy "shares with scientific management the assumptions of rationality and economic conceptions of humans . . . but economic gain is under the control of the organization and the person is to be engineered and controlled by the organization" (Sergiovanni et al., 1980).

It is convenient at this stage to examine the school in terms of Weber's dimensions of bureaucracy. Administrators attempt to bring order into schools and school systems through goals which are frequently set externally. Consequently, they search for the most efficient ways to achieve the goals; often they tend to overlook the human side. Some principals are seldom seen outside the office. To some extent, many difficulties of the 1960's and 1970's in schools were reactions to over-regulated, rule-oriented organizations determined to be efficient.

2.41 The School as a Bureaucracy

To examine the school as a bureaucratic organization, we will consider the above characteristics individually. Schools and school systems meet all the criteria, with the possible exception of the fourth (impersonality of relationships). If one were able to quantify the criteria, high "scores" on the dimensions would indicate a highly bureaucratic organizational structure, low scores otherwise.

Specialization. With bureaucracies, specialization has increased greatly in recent years. This is true in particular within school systems, with their superintendents of program, personnel, professional development, buildings, as well as many others, and co-ordinators, consultants, specialists in every subject. Secondary schools are structured around the subject department and the teachers with specialist qualifications in a large array of subjects. Some schools that have tried to organize around somewhat different criteria (for example, grouping of departments, house plans) have, in the main, been frustrated by the regulations and teachers' federations, jealous of the present salary qualifications system. In Ontario, however, an amendment to Regulation 262, in 1982, made it possible for secondary schools to be organized by "subject departments or other organizational units." Before, the last phrase was "other similar organizational units." Elementary schools, when based upon the self-contained classroom, had much less specialization among teachers, but in recent times, they too have a proliferation of specialists, including itinerant teachers of music, physical education and French, as well as other characteristics of the bureaucratic structure. An increased emphasis on special education has further fragmented the teaching staff into specialist categories; indeed, some provinces require teachers to be properly qualified with suitable specialist qualifications. Gue (1977) notes that the "growth of central office units of educational systems has also produced a division of labor and administrative specialization; quite apart from teaching qualifications."

Moreover, administrative functions have increasingly been separated from teaching functions. Superintendents never teach; principals, except in small schools, rarely.

Hierarchy of Authority. The hierarchical arrangement of offices is quite evident in the school and school system. It begins with the minister of education and runs all the way to the youngest pupil. Acts, regulations, circulars, memoranda, all set out positions within the hierarchy. The pupil must be obedient to the teacher, the teacher must perform the tasks assigned by the principal, the superintendent may assume all the authority of the principal, and so on. Many schools and school systems have a formal chart of authority. (One observes, however, that seldom are pupils mentioned in the organizational charts.) As noted earlier, however, the arrival of collective bargaining between boards and federations has muddied the waters somewhat; it may take some time before a new relationship is worked out in practice. This could be the first step away from the bureaucratic structure.

Rules, Regulations, and Policies. The basic "rule" is legislative—the various acts of the legislature and the regulations made under them. These cover almost all people taking part in education: pupils, teachers, principals, supervisory officers, boards of education, officials of the ministry, including the minister. Gilbert *et al.* (1982) explain the impact of this array of legal prescriptions upon the teacher. The teachers must also follow school policies, teachers' federation policies, and local conventions and customs.

The school policy manual might appear intimidating, but it does contain much useful information for the teacher; it also helps to put each person in the appropriate spot in the hierarchy.

An Impersonal Orientation in Relationships. The bureaucrat is expected to make rational decisions based on facts and according to the rules, to treat everyone with impartiality and equality, without personal feelings interfering. Is this possible in schools? Schools might appear to be organizations devoted to caring, personal relations, with decisions based on compassion rather than reason. Nevertheless, the rational, formal approach is part of the professional model of organization; so, in principle, there is no conflict here. Some authorities, however, believe that schools are more impersonally oriented than is generally thought. Sergiovanni *et al.* (1971), for example, state that the school has made extensive use of the principle of impartiality, for

> authority has been established on the basis of rational considerations rather than charismatic qualities or traditional imperatives; interpersonal interactions have tended to be functionally specific rather than functionally diffuse and official relationships have been governed largely by universalistic as contrasted with particularitistic considerations.

Careers Based on Competence. In the ideal bureaucracy, employment constitutes a full-time career and is based upon technical competence for the job. Promotion is also based upon competence as judged by superiors in the hierarchy of authority. Loyalty to the organization is most important and is secured with tenure and safeguards against arbitrary dismissal. Teachers fulfil these conditions quite well. Generally, they are appointed because they have the appropriate qualifications. Once the probationary period is over, dismissal can be made only for cause. Some collective bargaining agreements protect against unjust termination of contract, and all teachers have the right to appeal to the minister of education for a board of reference if they believe they have been unjustly dismissed. Strong teachers' federations keep a watchful eye on benefits like pensions and sick-leave provisions so that they are not arbitrarily changed or removed.

2.42   Problems of Bureaucracy

Weber's bureaucracy was designed as an efficient organization based upon the principles discussed above. Nevertheless, actions by administrators and others within the structure can have unintended and unanticipated consequences. It is as necessary for teachers to know about possible sources of conflict as to know the basic principles of the bureaucracy. Weber himself did not deal at any length with the disadvantages of a bureaucracy. Specialization, for example, can lead to boredom and the frustration of management's objectives when subordinates adopt their own norms and values. Of course, it is difficult to see teaching being so specialized into routines that it becomes boring. It could happen in some jurisdictions, especially those with closely regimented curricula and methods. When the enforcement of rules becomes an end in itself, it is easy to forget the original intention behind the rule. The principal, staff and pupils, where reasonable, should examine the school rules and their enforcement. One benefit of the agitation of the 1960's and 1970's was the examination of many rules that had been slavishly followed for years. Rules are necessary; the reasons for their existence should be clear. They should help achieve goals.

Problems result when achievement is not rewarded as it should be because of tenure and seniority. Often the salary grids for teachers are based upon paper qualifications; the only real extrinsic reward for achievement is promotion. A paradox — reward excellence in the classroom by promoting the teacher out of the classroom into a desk job. In some jurisdictions (for example, England and Wales) teachers may move up a salary scale without additional qualifications, but even this kind of action raises the question of who chooses and on what basis. Teachers in Canada, generally speaking, feel safer with the present approach. However, this system can affect attitudes towards innovations. Even when promotion of able teachers is a just reward, it frequently causes grumbling and discontent if some "hot-shot" becomes a department head or vice-principal after just a few years' service.

One mistaken notion about bureaucracy defines it as a slow and inefficient, bumbling structure. Myths like this frequently arise when a bureaucracy malfunctions. For example, the rigid adherence to rules, discussed above as a form of goal displacement, is the basis for the common phrase "red tape," — that somewhere in the process, procedures have ground to a halt because no one will move quickly and perhaps by-pass the rules. The low-level bureaucrat, let it be said, has no business chang-ing rules for individuals; fixed procedures were built into the bureau-cracy to eliminate favoritism. Sometimes, when people blame "red tape", they do so because they are really only looking for special treatment.

In this respect, incidentally, Weber's concept can be improved. It was noted earlier that the bureaucracy was a kindred spirit to scientific man-agement and, as such, lacked concern for the human side and overlooked the place of informal groups within the organization. The human rela-tions development showed the importance of this human side; a strictly functional bureaucracy could well have problems with morale. People in a bureaucracy may follow group norms rather than established practices, or else may be concerned with their own positions within the hierarchy; in both cases, it is the clients who may suffer.

Nevertheless, bureaucracies abound and it is necessary to come to terms with them. The structure serves an almost indispensable function in the daily round. Delays and seemingly inexplicable decisions are annoying, but on the whole, bureaucracy enables many jobs to be done and decisions to be made.

2.5   The Professional Organization

"Professionalism" can mean many things but most sources agree upon a core:

- Professionals possess a unique body of knowledge with specialized skills.
- Professionals are dedicated to serve their clients and make decisions about their welfare in accord with up-to-date knowledge.
- Professionals are committed to their work and constantly strive for competence.
- The professional person's authority is sanctioned by the community.
- Members of the profession follow an ethical code and standards of conduct.
- There is a professional culture, related to specialized knowledge and technical competence.
- The professional's conduct and competence are judged by a body composed of peers, with respect to licensing, discipline and admis-sion.

It is clear that many occupations are called "professional"; there are "professional" athletes, for example, as distiguished from the "amateurs." It is obvious also jobs can be arranged on a continuum of sorts. Most people would agree that physicians and surgeons, lawyers, dentists are professional people, while unskilled and semi-skilled laborers are not.

The other workers come somewhere in between. Some aspire to professionalism, others do not; some have it ascribed to them, whether they want it or not. Medicine, law, religious studies fit the criteria listed above. But is the teacher a professional? Perhaps too much can be made of the debate over details of professionalism; nevertheless, it is important that teachers understand the other side to organizational structure and the way professionalism affects their conduct in the staff-room and in the classroom.

Below are seven characteristics of the professional.

A unique Body of Knowledge. Members of a profession possess a unique body of knowledge based upon a systematic theory. They also have the technical skills necessary to put that knowledge into practice. Preparation for entry into the profession is a lengthy process and combines academic rigour with experience. But teachers cannot claim a unique body of knowledge. Most of their knowledge is based upon other disciplines. Some justification for the claim can be made about educational foundations, still in comparative infancy and labelled as off-shoots of other disciplines, for example, educational administration, educational psychology and sociology of education. Admittedly, technical competence is found in the teaching act in the classroom. It could be called unique to some extent, but this too is not so clearly drawn.

Teachers and administrators have problems deciding just what the characteristics of good teaching are. If there is a technical competence, it should be reasonable to expect that it could be described and teachers evaluated accordingly. Such an authority as J. M. Paton (1975) with many years' experience as a teacher, administrator, federation official, professor and author noted that "the most recent available references indicate that educational research has failed so far to define, to detect reliably, or to evaluate competence in teaching."

On this particular dimension, it is apparent that teachers do not rate highly. There is no cause for pessimism, however. The increasing research into knowledge and methods is perceptibly, albeit slowly, edging teaching in the direction of a unique body of knowledge. Teachers who believe themselves professionals should do all they can to support these efforts, by taking an interest in research in their own fields and by increasing their own knowledge and technical know-how.

Orientation towards Clients. Professionals try to serve the interests of clients in the best way possible, if necessary to the detriment of their own interests. It is tacitly assumed that the clients in the relationships lack the knowledge with which to judge the professionals' actions. The professionals, in return, do not recommend services that the clients do not need.

The teachers and principal in a school would try to act in the best interests of their clients, the pupils in the school. Teachers would not normally recommend unnecessary homework or courses. Of course, the school has other sets of clients, the parents and the community at large. Towards the former, the teachers adopt "professional" attitudes. The same would normally be the case towards the community as well, although sometimes the school might make political or convenient decisions regarding the curriculum, or mechanical arrangements such as site-selection or special amenities. Perhaps, those political decisions ought to be made by trustees; few, if any, have argued that trustees are professionals. In any case, many of the decisions about clients are prescribed by regulations or custom.

Commitment to Work and Excellence. Professionals devote much time to their work and to keeping up with developments. This inevitably means that they devote long hours to the job above and beyond the nominal time allotted. They are not content to get by with what was learnt in university, but continue to take courses to upgrade their qualifications and to learn more about their subjects or their teaching methods; they also read professional journals and take an interest in research.

Professional Activity Days are helpful here. Many teachers take part enthusiastically, some do not. As the popular public view of professional activity days is not flattering, teachers could improve their public image by demonstrating that they are devoting the time to their work and striving for excellence.

Authority Sanctioned by the Community. Professionals are accorded a status because the community believes that their special skills give them the right to make decisions that will, in general, be followed individually and collectively. Before state licensing, professionals had formed their own organizations, whose decisions were accepted by the community. To some extent, the state has moved in to give public approval; indeed, it could be argued that in allowing professional bodies to set their own standards, the state is merely reinforcing the community sanction. Teachers enjoy community sanction, depending upon the school, the nature of the community, and the cultural background. But the state, in licensing teachers, imposed its own standards on those seeking admission to teaching.

Private schools also enjoy community sanction of authority. Principals, headmasters and headmistresses do not require formal principal's qualifications, yet their authority, in a professional sense, is not challenged by their clients. The professional in any field enjoys a "high level of public trust and confidence" (Sergiovanni *et al.*, 1980).

Code of Conduct. As a result of long training and exposure to the profession, professionals are expected to understand the ethics of the profession. These may be written down, or passed on, or both. They will also work under the close scrutiny of peers, who will see that they adhere to the standards.

This is true for teachers. The provincial teachers' federation have their codes of ethics where the various duties of members are spelled out. In addition, during teaching practice at a college or faculty of education and during the early years of teaching, more experienced teachers help the beginner. The matter of ethics and conduct spills over into the discussion of self-licensing, which will be discussed below.

A Professional Culture. In addition to a body of knowledge and technical know-how, each profession has its culture, based on knowledge, ethics, customs and technical jargon. To some extent, it helps keep the public mystified and thus aids community sanction. On the other hand, it also helps in professional communications and clarity of expression.

Teachers do not possess a great mystique; too many pople have been to school. Their jargon is not well developed and their customs are not particularly unique. In this characteristic, they do not appear to be at the professional end of the continuum.

Self-licensing of a Profession. The professional organization is quite unlike a hierarchical organization, and exercises a different control. Professionals have traditionally had their own associations which admit persons to practise the particular profession, and issue licences and discipline members. In recent years, statutes have been enacted which give the various bodies the legal right to continue to carry out these traditional tasks. Newnham and Nease (1970) write:

> The statutes by which a profession is recognized constitute a contract between the profession and the state. The enactment, which is the legal foundation of a profession, makes it clear to the members of the profession that the public, as represented by the government, recognizes them as possessing certain skills and standards.

In Ontario, for example, the medical profession has a three-fold structure. The universities prepare members for admission by granting university degrees. The Ontario College of Physicians and Surgeons, under the Ontario Medical Act, is the only licensing authority; it has the power to discipline members, including the right to strike a member off the register, that is, to take away the licence. The Ontario Medical Association (OMA) is devoted to the advancement of professional aims and ideals, as well as the welfare of members. In a recent (1982) dispute about fees and payment under the Ontario Hospital Insurance Plan (OHIP), it was the OMA that bargained with the government of Ontario.

For the legal profession, the model is quite similar, except that lawyers were not always prepared by a university; they had their own Law schools, combined with on-the-job preparation. Since Osgoode Hall (the law school) affiliated with York University, its graduates now receive degrees from that institution. The admission, licensing and disciplinary body in Ontario is the Upper Canada Law Society; the professional organization is the Bencher's Society.

The clergy, the third group of the traditional professions, are prepared either at universities or in theological colleges which have their own charters or acts establishing them. They are admitted to the practice by their own religious denominations in various ways, depending upon the particular organizational structure concerned. This process entitles the clergy to use the titles "reverend" or "rabbi" or whatever else is appropriate; in all cases, the titles are sanctioned by the public and further legitimated by various acts of the legislature. In addition, the positions of the ordained clergy carry with them certain state functions, such as the legal solemnization of marriages.

Teachers in Ontario undergo training similar to those in the traditional professions; that is, they are prepared in a university, in a combination of classroom and practical work. This model was not always the case; only in the early 1970's did a university degree become a prerequisite for entering teaching. The last teachers' college was closed in 1979; the others had joined various universities, and some had previously been closed. At this point, however, the model varies from those of medicine and the law: although there is a Teaching Profession Act and an Ontario Teachers' Federation (both of which will be discussed later), the teachers have no licensing body corresponding to the College of Physicians and Surgeons or the Law Society. The minister grants certificates under authority given by the Education Act. The minister establishes a board of reference to settle disputes between a teacher and the employing board over a termination of contract.

In 1980, the Ontario minister of education, Dr. Bette Stephenson, stated that it was time that teachers became a self-licensing profession. Since 1982, various groups, including the Ontario Teachers' Federation, have been studying the proposal.

Many professional groups have licensing bodies; some are under the jurisdiction of a government department, others not. Some professions and even quasi-professions can insist that all those doing the task be licensed; others have not yet achieved that level. For example, the public generally agrees that professional engineers have special skills that make them more or less indispensable. Librarians, on the other hand, are not regarded like that. In some provinces, the library board need appoint only one professional librarian, for any size of system. In practice, many, but not all, "librarians" hold university degrees and certificates as professional librarians issued by the appropriate minister.

The teacher, then, is in the position of being what Etzioni (1964) labels a "quasi-professional," quite professional on some of the dimensions discussed, but less so on others. What is certain, however, is that in almost all schools, publicly and privately supported, the teachers work in a bureaucratically structured organization, a structure which conflicts in many ways with the concept of the professional organization.

Weber believed that collegiality obstructs efficient decision-making and prevents consistency of policy because professionals want to make their own decisions. This situation can be avoided by concentrating power in the hands of a few. The school, in some respects, follows this model: a group of people with professional orientations, working within an organization where the official authority is concentrated in one person at the top.

2.6   Reactions to the Bureaucratic/Professional Conflict

There are two significant conflicts. The first exists because administrators and teachers have different expectations: the administrators see the teachers as lower-level bureaucrats, while the teachers aspire towards increasing professionalism. The second conflict occurs when the teachers must decide whether to accept the more bureaucratic orientation or to fulfil their professional aspirations.

In the first case, the supervisory nature of the senior administrator's function recalls the hierarchical nature of the bureaucracy. There, those in higher offices have more expertise than, and hence are able to supervise, those in lower offices. This conflict is exacerbated when supervisory officers or principals with little expertise in a certain subject must evaluate teachers with considerable experience and qualifications. Many teachers want to become more professional by helping to make decisions and by taking a greater interest in their subjects. Corwin (1965) noted in a study of conflict between administrators and teachers, that the more professional the orientation of teachers, the greater the conflict. About 25 per cent of the conflicts studied were over issues of authority. Corwin concluded that there "is a consistent pattern of conflict between teachers and administrators over the control of work and that professionalization is a militant process." Since Corwin wrote those words, teachers have become more militant. Some of this militance is left-wing politics but by-and-large, it is evidence of a greater desire by teachers to share in decision-making in the school and the school system. Newnham and Nease (1970) predicted this trend when they wrote:

> The professional teacher, relying on his developing competence, is beginning to demand autonomy in his teaching and with it he expects to assume responsibility for his decisons and actions. Similarly, individual schools are beginning to demand autonomy in developing a program of studies for their students, thus creating at a different level a further area of conflict between themselves and the central authority.

Collective bargaining pushed teachers, through their federations, into areas (like class sizes, number of teaching periods) long considered sacrosanct by trustees and supervisory officers. Now teachers have a greater say in the day-to-day running of schools. Some gains have been made at the expense of the power held by principals. Many principals believe they are losing their authority on all sides; this may be a step backwards from their point of view, but no doubt also a step towards increasing collegiality.

The teachers' federations also seek job security for their members. Herein lies another source of conflict for the further professionalization of teachers.

The second significant conflict is that which afflicts individual teachers. What are the teachers' reactions when they face the bureaucratic/ professional dichotomy? Gouldner (1957) studied conflict between professional and organizational commitment in a small private liberal-arts college. He identified two main attitudes, to which he attached the labels "cosmopolitan" and "local." (It is not only in teaching that the conflict occurs, for the number of salaried professionals in all fields has been growing steadily.) Gouldner (1957) defined the terms as follows:

Cosmopolitans—low on loyalty to the organization, high on commitment to specialized skills and likely to use an external reference group.

Locals—high on loyalty to the organization, low on commitment to specialized skills and likely to use an internal reference group.

In his subsequent analysis of the data, Gouldner (1958) developed six sub-groups for "locals" and two for "cosmopolitans."

Dedicated locals are complete insiders and accept totally the goals of the organization. They form an inner reference group and believe implicitly in the bureaucratic values.

True bureaucrat locals resist all efforts at outside control. They are concerned with the continuity of the organization and its hierarchical nature. They follow rules and obey orders without questions. No doubt there are teachers like this. For them, the principal is boss and is always right; the superintendent possesses powers not unlike those of Superman or Wonderwoman.

Homeguard locals are distinguished from the others by their commitment to the organization because they themselves attended it, or married into it. They are committed to the organization because they feel comfortable with it. In schools, this phenomenon occurs in the older, established, private schools. Former students as staff members are also common in smaller centres and, before the rapid expansion of the 1960's, common in big-city schools, secondary schools in particular because there were relatively fewer of them.

Elder locals are completely committed to the organization and its values, as long as they remain as they were in the past. They evaluate everything in those terms. Schools had many elder locals before the mobility of the 1960's. It was a mark of distinction to have served in the same school for 35 years, even in the same classroom. No one doubted what values such a teacher stood for. Stability was the result. With the increasing mobility of teachers and a rapid growth of numbers, elder locals declined in relative number and influence. But now, with declining enrolment, lack of mobility and increasing stability, perhaps we shall see some again. A combination of militancy and forced rotations of principalships and vice-principalships (that is as far as it goes at present) militate against any grand revival. It takes time to build a cadre of elders, in any case.

Outsider cosmopolitans are part of the organization in theory, but not committed to it in practice. They have strong outside commitments connected to their areas of expertise. They get their intellectual stimuli from the outside sources, not from the organization. In schools, such outsiders frequently remain apart from the staff; for example, they eat lunch together, perhaps in back rooms, and they try to escape staff meetings whenever possible by pleading (truthfully) other professional commitments. They read the principal's memoranda and follow them insofar as they do not conflict with their own personal professional views. It takes a strong principal to bring them to heel, and the fight is probably not worth it.

Empire-builder cosmopolitans are integrated into the organization up to a point; that is, they accept the established order of things, but battle away for more autonomy and a greater say for their own (collective) sub-division of the organization. In a school, this could be a strong subject department under a strong department head. Because members of a department frequently teach in proximity to each other and meet in a formally designated place (departmental office), it is not surprising that such cliques exist. The subject orientation in some faculties of education and elsewhere encourages this attitude. The competent, skilful practitioners start to believe in the overwhelming importance of their own subject; a state of affairs magnified by physical proximity, formal certification requirements and tradition. In any organization, they are an important force to deal with, particularly when sweeping changes are contemplated. Empire builders, as history shows, are difficult to turn aside, no matter how virtuous and sincere they are.

Presthus (1962) provides a second perspective on the bureaucratic/professional conflict. He wrote of the ways those in bureaucratic organizations cope with tensions within the organization and of the ways they view ambition. These he categorized into three types.

Upward mobiles generally accept the organization, warts and all. They embrace the goals and organizational values and approve of superordinates. They believe in hierarchical authority and all that comes with it. *Indifferents,* although they accept the reality of the organization, are not deeply committed to it and find their satisfaction elsewhere. The job provides the means to enjoy the finer things in life. *The ambivalents* accept the attractions of power and authority but value their own independence. They want to be their "own man" or "woman," not to be a "company man" or "woman." They value their own sense of individuality which, they believe, does not fit the bureaucratic mould.

All three of Presthus' types can be found in a school system; indeed, it is possible that any one given person, over time, can become two or even all three types. The "hotshots" do everything according to the rules, take the right graduate courses, run a tight ship and get their reports in on time and, at least in better times, are rewarded with a vice-principalship or some kind of headship or chairmanship. For a few of these upward mobiles, the prize turns out to be a hollow victory when their genuine attempts to better themselves and their schools face bureaucratic obstinacy. They see that the emperor has no clothes and retreat to a position of ambivalence. Some become private consultants, some become consultants with the ministry of education, some become officers in teachers' federations, while still others join faculties of education. Many soldier on, frustrated.

The remainder toil on as indifferents, getting the job done and achieving satisfaction. For them the weekend is a welcome rest and holidays are spent as holidays, not on upgrading courses. The upward mobiles approve; the more indifferents there are, the less the competition.

Presthus (1962) doubted that there were many ambivalents. Owen (1981) claims, however, that:

> we have recently observed an increase in the number of teachers who are, organizationally speaking, ambivalent, and who have challenged well-established practices such as the primacy of administrators, the status traditionally associated with "promotion" from teaching to administration, and the rewards customarily reserved for administration.

Perhaps, as the job-squeeze tightens and promotions become fewer, the teachers' federations will become more involved in the daily operation of schools. The branch or local president (shop steward) is the one whom principals must consult and with whom administrators must interpret the collective bargaining agreement. It is becoming a new position of power in the hierarchy of the school system.

People behave according to their aspirations, motivations, and frustrations, and in response to leadership, changes, attitudes and decision-making. This is true for both the teachers and the pupils.

2.7   Post-Weberian Bureaucracy

Although the bureaucratic model has greatly influenced the schools, other structures are also important. March and Simon (1958) note that "while Weber perceived bureaucracy as an adaptive device for using specialized skills, he is not exceptionally attentive to the character of the human organism."

The work of Talcott Parsons serves as an example of contemporary sociology. He views the organization in terms of its control over the activities of the members of the organization. Parsons (1949) attempted to show in his organizational model how a network of interdependent systems and subsystems meet each other's needs; the "central value system" in a society; and the definable role-expectations that predict behaviour, thus permitting a stable society.

According to Parsons, it is necessary to know what goals or values an organization has before it can be analysed. In later writings (1960), he describes organizations as societies on a small scale, and organizational goals as an extension of survival needs in society. Parsons is a prolific writer, and it is not possible to consider his contribution in greater detail. His approach has become known as the "theory of action," which holds that action is oriented to or influenced by others and that their behaviour is taken into account. It is used to construct a systematic explanation of human behaviour.

Parsons writes in terms of social and cultural systems, of links between systems, and of the need for organizations to become efficient and stable. He describes two changes: "exogenous", caused by external environmental influences; and "endogenous", caused by internal factors. His "central value system," which is the product of the society where the organization flourishes, influences change. The central value system determines the goals of the organization. Parsons (1959) suggests that the goal of the school, as a social system, is to teach children the value of "individualistic achievement"; its structure and processes are related to this goal.

He writes as a structural-functionalist, that is, from the point of view of functions rather than causes of change. The structuralists generally try to bridge the conflict between the classical and human relations perspectives. They recognize the stresses produced in the many dichotomous situations arising within organizations. They went beyond the study of business and industrial organizations to examine many others: churches, armies, schools and hospitals. Thus they indirectly prepared the development of a deeper understanding of the school as an organization. As a result of the work of the action school, organizational analysis now includes:

- Both formal and informal elements of the organization and their articulation
- The scope of informal groups and relations between such groups inside and outside the organization
- Both higher and lower ranks
- Both social and material rewards and their effects on each other
- The interaction between the organization and its environment
- Both work and non-work organizations

(Etzioni, 1964)

Although analysing functions is not the only way in which to view an organization, the functionalist approach provides an orderly framework.

The organizational analysis now also embraces the examination of causes of and reactions to internal and external influences. From the point of view of educational administration, this effect itself is a sufficient reason to make the study of the functionalists important. For so long, the schools operated as if in a world by themselves. Conant (1959) noted that university professors who criticized the secondary school believed it "operated in a social vacuum." They assumed all children came equally well prepared and with similar backgrounds, all enjoyed school to the same extent, and all went home having been equally stimulated, to parents all interested in what had occurred. Husen (1979) points out that "this is, indeed, wishful thinking that ignores the social framework of the school, which has to serve children from a rich variety of backgrounds, children from *all* families, not only my children and the children of my friends."

Small wonder then that new concepts of organizations and administration led to increased understanding of the relations and activities within the school.

One of the organizational psychologists, Silverman (1970) suggested that the human relations approach in business organizations fell short because it assumed that no real conflict of interest existed between the worker and the employer. Wilensky (1957) was concerned about the lack of attention paid to external factors like union activity, personal ambition, mobility, and local conditions. Organizational psychologists began to realize that underestimation of this conflict is a serious matter. Maslow suggests that needs increase once basic physiological needs are met.

Silverman (1970) lists the following premises of organizational psychologists:

- Varying needs and motives exert a direct influence on behaviour. Behaviour is explained when the needs upon which it is based are known.
- The needs of individuals conflict with the goals of organizations. The conflict is best resolved by changing the organizational structure.
- The best organization responds to individual and organizational needs by encouraging stable work groups and participation in decision-making, and by establishing non-bureaucratic structures that set objectives rather than a hierarchy of authority.

Silverman designed this list of premises for the study of industrial organizations; nevertheless, it applies just as well to schools. Many principals and supervisory officers ignore the first premise; that is, they still assume schools operate in vacuums and therefore ignore the problems of staff and pupils when formulating policies.

The second premise has many overtones; it is not the place here to follow the political ramifactions but some left-wing teachers' organizations indeed believe the whole structure must be changed.

The third premise calls for more participation by the "followers" in decisions made by "leaders." Even now, at some school staff meetings, the principal stands at the front and all the teachers sit in rows and nod agreement at the appropriate moments. The organizational psychologists quite plainly saw a greater role for the professional in a bureaucratic structure. Because of legislation and regulations, and the traditions of education in Canada, however, it will be some time before these views could be implemented in a broad fashion. Still, some enlightened supervisory officers and principals are encouraging the teachers to take part.

The needs of those in organizations can be studied by using two approaches as examples: social man and self-actualization.

Social man. Continuing the work of Roethlisberger and Dickson, Mayo (1945) found that work is a group activity; the social life of the adult is built around it; a sense of belonging is more important than physical conditions; and the norms of informal groups have a strong effect upon the individual. His findings ignore many factors, such as unions and professional norms, and attitudes of the consumer. In schools, two informal groups may arise—one among teachers, and the other among pupils. Do the needs and norms of one exist at the expense of those of the other? The teachers, in their quasi-professional roles, may be caught between professional obligation to their discipline and the goals set by management. Such a situation does not normally occur in industrial organizations.

According to Homans (1950), the organization comprises two basic divisions: the formal organization and all its trappings, and the informal group structure. He saw merit in allowing these informal groups to have some part in decision-making. It was up to the group leader to achieve the goals of the group and to maintain a balance of incentives to encourage the obedience of the followers.

Psychologists are still studying the small group within the organization. The importance of the small group within a school or university is considerable.

Self-actualization. Maslow (1954) argued that, in addition to the basic needs, there was a higher need, that of self-actualization or the realization of one's full potential. In his hierarchy of needs, as one need is satisfied, the next higher becomes the source of concern and motivation.

Whether his "needs" are real or not has not been determined; he himself calls them "instinctoid." He speculated that perhaps very few actually achieve the higher levels of his hierarchy. What might be "needs" in one culture might not be in another, or they may not exist at all. He assumes that some universal set pre-exists the participants. The schema has had appeal as a model to explain behaviour and to develop hypotheses.

Getzels and Guba (1958) combined the formal structure and the needs of individuals and groups into a social process model. This comprised a nomothetic dimension (the institution, the role and expectations) and an idiographic dimension (the individual's personality and needs—disposition). The interaction of these, in particular the role and the personality, accounts for the observed behaviour of people within an institution. Getzels and Guba used this model to hypothesize about role-personality conflicts, from which Guba (1960) decided that "the unique task of the administrator can now be understood as that of mediating between these two sets of behaviour-eliciting forces, that is, the nomothetic and the idiographic."

McGregor (1960) pushed the two dimensions even further. He labelled them Theory X and Theory Y. The first held that people dislike work; they want security and will only work towards objectives if given economic incentives. This was Taylor's position and of those who see a "good" school as one that emphasizes drill, punishments, obedience, combined with a system of tangible rewards (prizes, honours, prefect systems). The alternative resembles Maslow's hierarchy of needs; that is, that workers work towards organizational objectives for the intangible reward of ego-satisfaction and self-actualization. It is the manager's responsibility to see that this is possible.

Argyris (1957) writes that conflict between the needs of the individual and the demands of the organization is inevitable, it is management's task to minimize this conflict. One method is to build trust so that no one is threatened. Another is to let all participants establish goals to which all can subscribe.

2.8   Abstract Theory: The Systems and Phenomenological Approaches

The systems approach is based on the assumption that system is ontologically prior to action and that system pre-exists and to some extent constrains the individual through its structure and expectations. It is, in essence, the acceptance of a role determined externally. Greenfield (1975) notes it in stating:

In common parlance we speak of organizations as if they were real. Neither scholar nor layman finds difficulty with talk in which organizations serve functions, adapt to their environments, clarify their goals, or act to implement policy.

The other component of the systems approach is the premise that social reality is a natural order which gives reason to human society. Organization provides an order and stability within which people work. This organization is likened to an organism; it exists and has its own characteristics, and a life cycle based upon the theory of the survival of the fittest.

Systems theory has played a large part in the study of organizations in recent years, especially in the study of schools and educational administration.

According to the systems approach, the role of theory is to explain how social reality might be changed. It uses the analogy of the physical sciences; theory explains what already exists in fact. This view entails complex research to confirm theories of what might be expected. These attempts frequently include mathematical models to find relations between variables. The common criticism of these models is that they are either remote from reality or trivial. Other criticisms are that they depend on the isolation of variables (which is difficult enough) and there is often no guarantee that all variables have been accounted for. The analogy with the physical sciences is tenuous, but the appeal to a fundamental set of rules is difficult to ignore. Whether these rules are universally acceptable is another matter; what is fundamental to one group may not be to another.

The systems model has been used for thirty years to study political, educational and marketing organizations. This model is like an organization of interrelated and interdependent parts that form a whole, and is used to study more complex phenomena. A general systems theory can be used to emphasize the similarities found in different relationships.

Systems theory is built upon functionalism, that is, an approach that sees similarities between biological organisms and social organizations.

Allport (1955) offered a comprehensive definition:

A system, in other words, is something that is concerned with some kind of activity, and preserves a kind of integration and unity; and a particular system can be recognized as distinct from other systems to which, however, it may be dynamically related. Systems may be complex; they may be made up of interdependent subsystems, each of which, though less autonomous than the entire aggregate, is nevertheless fairly distinguishable in operation.

A major assumption is that the model is an accurate analogy of reality, and so can explain the different organisms and organizations. The functioning of parts is determined by the system as a whole, that is, the organization affects individual actions within the system.

Systems theory holds that organizations also exhibit behaviour that can be observed in repeating patterns; the analogy to an organism is strong. Reification is well advanced and must be carefully regarded lest all actions of individuals be ignored, as for example, in the case of the modification of formal positions within an organization by the individual characteristics of the actors themselves.

Griffiths (1964) proposed three types of relationships with the environment:

- A closed system that makes no exchanges with its supra-system
- An open system that interacts both up and down; with degrees of open-ness and closed-ness
- When nothing enters the system, it will run down to a state of equilibrium, with no conclusion

The closed system is completely independent of its environment. It adheres rigidly to organizational goals; it is not affected by the environment. Open systems have recognizable relationships with their environments. According to Griffiths (1964) they have the following characteristics:

- They tend to maintain themselves in a steady state.
- They are self-regulating.
- They produce identical results from different initial conditions.
- They maintain their steady states in part through the interplay of subsystems.
- They maintain their steady states in part by responding to contributions.

The open system can be divided into parts: the environment is the suprasystem; the organization, the system; and the parts within it, the subsystem.

The open system has the advantage of showing how an organization becomes stable by taking advantage of its environment. The description closely follows the organic model, and some differences: boundaries and relations between parts are not as well defined. The behaviour of people (the elements) causes changes in relations. Social systems are not "born" in the same sense that organisms are but they do form agreements. The differing behaviour makes relationships less predictable, and perhaps even allows conflicts among them (Katz and Kahn, 1956). Sub-system elements accept the norms of the system. If they do not, conflict may occur between goals set by different levels within the organization.

Malfunctions within an open system are corrected by an adjustment or a reaction. The structure can be changed to fit new needs. There is the further analogy in the adoption of a pseudo-change, or a facade, in order to ward off predators. Whether this is in reaction to a threat, or is a deliberate result of an internal decision is difficult to determine in the case of a social system; the systems view may not hold completely.

The major criticism of the systems approach, writes Hoyle (1976), is that "it gives ontological priority to the abstract properties of organization, over the actions of those who 'people' them at any given time." In other words, the organization as a reified concept is more important than the actions of the people who are governed by the properties. On the other hand, an organization is more than the mere presence of the individual participants, but whether the reification of the organization is justified on these grounds is another matter. There is comfort in accepting an institutionalized role when joining an organization. One knows what to expect.

Phenomenology. It is beyond the scope of this work to give more than a brief description of phenomenology to show its impact on "traditional" sociological thinking. Modern phenomenology arose in the early part of this century; both the "idealists" and "realists" shared an interest in the problem of consciousness: "for as a disclosure of the world ... phenomenology's task was to reveal the mystery of the world and of reason" (Merleau-Ponty, 1962).

This task was accomplished by what Silverman (1972) describes as "an exploration of the obvious." The obvious is usually taken for granted; to begin an investigation is to question preconceptions about ordinary people as they go about their everyday lives, or the preconceptions of the scientist about the physical world or the actions of other people.

A phenomenological approach causes people to put to one side those views they hold, to abandon a "commonsense" or "everyone knows that" view, and to try to understand the usually accepting process of experiencing.

Sociologists using a phenomenological approach recognize a primary duty to develop an understanding of, and to describe, the subjective meanings of human action ... (they) must seek to understand the processes by which the actors in the situation make sense of it (Dale, 1973).

Phenomenological sociologists do not agree that organizations have goals or values or act as entities in some ordered fashion. The people within the organization determine events. But who shall prevail, if goals and values differ among individuals? A consensus must be reached before transactions can take place. If a conflict arises, then a solution must be found.

To resolve difficulties within the organization, change must take place not in the structure but in the beliefs held by individuals in it. Change in attitudes must take place first. To do this, it must first be known what sets of values are held, who holds which set, and which are in conflict.

In the phenomenological approach, theory follows, rather than precedes, research. The method best suited to this is the case study, which deals with individual people in specific situations. Measurement is not important, not even necessary; the understanding of relations is paramount. Rose (1962) writes that "this emphasis upon observation [and] on process distinguish the thought and researches of the interactionists from those of most followers of 'functional' theory in sociology."

How does one see how someone else makes sense? Hoyle (1976) suggests that if a sociologist tries to see from the outside what these "constructs of reality" are, reification looms up again.

Further examination is beyond the scope of this work; it is sufficient to describe its impact on the study of organizations. A useful paper is that of Greenfield (1975); he contrasts the systems and phenomenological views, with particular emphasis on the school. The relationship between phenomenology and the theme of this study is indirect, for it represents a way of getting at the fundamental question rather than being a system of relationships.

2.9   The School as a Social System

A school, a complex organization, has both formal and informal groups within it. Teachers and pupils belong to both. Each teacher has formal responsibilities: to teach certain classes, to work with certain other teachers. Most also belong to informal groups within the school: a car-pool, a coffee-making group, a lunch-room clique. Pupils, obviously, have similar connections.

New members are expected to replace the old and behave in accordance with established procedures. The Hawthorne experiments showed the importance of group norms. The organization chart describes the authority of one role over another. This "chart" may be an actual document (see page 42) or it may be implied in documentary form, in a regulation, for example, "a supervisory officer may...assume any of the authority and responsibilities of the principal."

Most administrators realize that formal organization charts are frequently only a façade (handy to fall back on when something goes wrong). The networks and groups within the formal chart frequently determine the making of decisions. Many teachers also realize the important roles are located in the intersection of the formal lattice-work and manage to get assigned important tasks to move upward. Although the organization chart can show roles, these are filled by people with different personalities; indeed, the more professional a role it is, the more scope for individual differences.

A teacher has many roles; Gue (1977) lists four social roles: staff member, contractor, buck receiver and supervisor. In addition, the teacher acts like a kind, firm and judicious parent (as a disciplinarian), a counsellor, a policeman, a judge, a coach, a learned professional, among other roles. Some roles conflict with one another. Within the informal structure, the teacher plays other roles. Principals must work with both the informal and formal groups to help teachers succeed and get along. The power of informal groups and leaders can be strong, and principals should be aware of them in order to make use of them. To be a leader, the principal must use the informal network to change group norms. The principal must know which groups exist, who is in them, and who are the informal leaders. Of course, a dissatisfied teacher belonging to more than one group can cause trouble. Again, the principal must be aware of the situation and take steps to change it.

Jacob Getzels and Egon Guba (1957) described the social system as "involving two major classes of phenomena, which are at once conceptually independent and phenomenally interactive. There are first, the *institutions* with certain roles and expectations that will fulfil the goals of the system, second, inhabiting the system are the *individuals* with certain *personalities* and *need-dispositions*, whose interactions comprise what we generally call social behaviour."

They note that both these dimensions supply motives; the social behaviour we observe is the result of interaction between these two sets of motives. To understand the behaviour of "specific role incumbents" in an organization, we must be able to recognize both the role expectations and need-dispositions. Their model enables us to see relationships. It is a useful model, popular among students of organizational structure. It is the theoretical basis of many studies of behaviour, especially of principals.

Scarboro—Board of Education
Organization Chart 1975-76

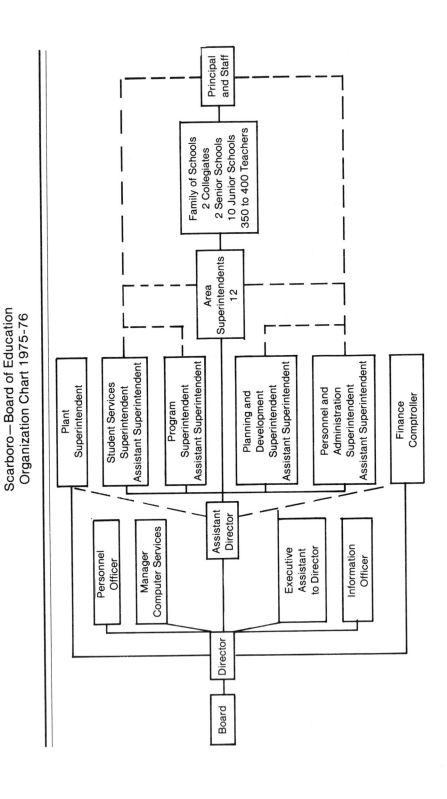

Appendix F
MSSB Organization

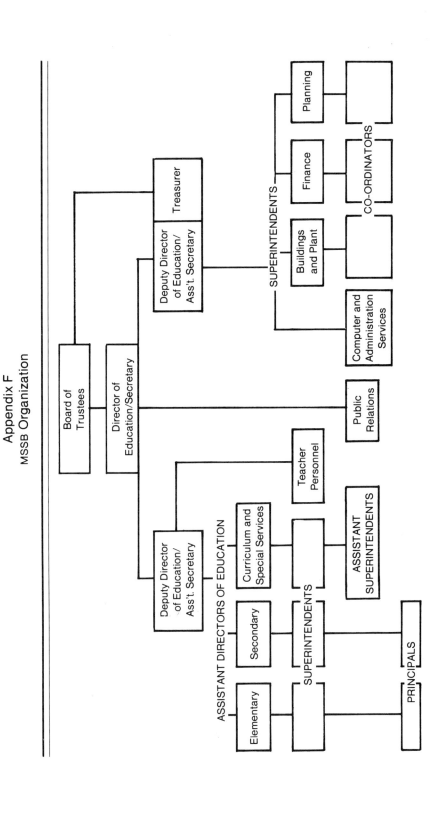

Board of Trustees

Director of Education/Secretary

Deputy Director of Education/ Ass't. Secretary

Treasurer

SUPERINTENDENTS

Buildings and Plant

Finance

Planning

CO-ORDINATORS

Computer and Administration Services

Public Relations

Deputy Director of Education/ Ass't. Secretary

ASSISTANT DIRECTORS OF EDUCATION

Elementary

Secondary

Curriculum and Special Services

Teacher Personnel

SUPERINTENDENTS

ASSISTANT SUPERINTENDENTS

PRINCIPALS

3 Leadership

3 Leadership

3.1 Analysis of Leadership

Leadership is most important in the study of a school or school system; the principals and supervisors are obviously leaders but so are teachers and, to some extent, pupils. Teachers must understand leadership to base their actions upon some well-established principles.

First, "administration" and "leadership" mean different things. The former usually means the carrying out of routine tasks. This is done along the lines of Gulick's POSDCORB. For a school principal, these duties would include preparing timetables, drawing up the budget, setting objectives, and working with parents and pupils' organizations. On the other hand, leadership is more than that; it includes the initiation of changes in structures, attitudes, and goals. The leader goes beyond routine and is always trying to influence the followers to try something different.

Sergiovanni *et al.* (1980) point out that "administration," in the research literature at least, is somehow inferior to "leadership." One should not have to choose between the two; both are important. No doubt, leaders — the principal or teacher — are still responsible for routine tasks. Some would wish it were not so, but many principals seem content to be administrators. In their study of educational leadership in Ontario, Gilbert *et al* (1977) noted that principals and vice-principals believed that they had been well prepared for the routine administrative tasks. On the other hand, they reported perceived relative deficiencies in other skills, particularly those involving interpersonal relationships.

A long-held idea is that leaders somehow have those undefinable characteristics that cause others to put them on a pedestal. Historical figures from Julius Caesar to Mao Tse Tung have all been studied for those individual traits; for example, intelligence, physical characteristics, social behaviour, and emotional stability. In his review, Stogdill (1948) concluded that the studies had failed to turn up any discernible correlation between leadership and personal characteristics. He made some generalizations, however:

- About 15 studies suggest that the average leader in a group, when compared with the average members, exceeds them in intelligence, scholarship, dependability, participation in social activities, and socio-economic status.
- The skills and characteristics found in a leader are to a large degree determined by the situation in which the leadership role is to be played.

It is apparent that physical characteristics play little part in the selection of school principals. There are tall principals, short principals, fat principals, thin principals. For many years, women were excluded; now, they are not.

Stogdill continued his studies for more than 25 years. In 1974, he published a further report on leadership qualities. He states that certain traits seem to produce "personality dynamics advantageous to the person seeking the responsibilities of leadership." He categorized the traits as self-oriented, task-related, and social. One cannot predict by these characteristics themselves who will be an effective leader.

The study of leadership then turned from the search for a theory of traits to an examination of the situations leaders find themselves. Admirable Crichton is the archetypal situational leader. He was a butler. When cast on a deserted island, however, he knew how to survive, and his erstwhile masters and mistresses followed his lead agreeably. After the rescue, all returned to "normal." Neither traits nor the situation is the whole answer, although both have some effect upon leadership. As Hoy and Miskel (1978) put it, "What traits, under what situations, are important to leader effectiveness?" The transactions between leader and followers are also important.

In 1939, Lewin, Lippit and White of the University of Iowa conducted a series of experiments. The study most widely known is that in which three groups of boys, about 10-12 years old and members of a hobby club, were given some handicraft tasks to accomplish. The boys were divided into groups, each one under the charge of adults who adopted different leadership styles labelled "autocratic," "democratic," and "laisse-faire."

In the democratic groups, the leaders sat down with the boys and discussed details of what would be done and how it would be done. They made suggestions, offered help, but the aim was to have the boys themselves make the final decisions. In the autocratic groups, the leaders arbitrarily imposed upon the members the decisions reached in the democratic groups. They allowed no discussion; the boys simply had to do as they were instructed. They handed out details from time-to-time and formed groups quite arbitrarily. The leaders remained aloof but friendly. The laissez-faire groups were left to their own devices; the leaders supplied instruction and materals for completing the job but remained passive, allowing questions to be asked, but volunteering nothing. They offered no praise or blame and mostly were not involved in the planning or the work.

It is informative to note the reactions when leaders left the groups alone for a time, then returned. In the autocratic groups, when the leaders left, pandemonium ensued. When the leaders returned, order was restored and tasks were eventually completed. In the laissez-faire groups, the boys generally left soon after the leaders, who returned to empty rooms and incomplete jobs.

The behaviour in the groups also varied greatly. In the democratic groups, the boys thought highly of their leaders; they talked of "our" models and "our group." Criticism was objective and the boys were proud of their work. In the autocratic groups, the boys showed much tension and aggressiveness — towards the leaders and each other. Rather than confront the leader, they chose a scapegoat to blame and they talked of strikes and downright destructiveness. The laissez-faire groups were also aggressive, but in a more diffused and chaotic way, rather than directed toward the leader. They did not really focus on anything at all, in either a positive or a negative sense.

What are the lessons to be learned from these studies? The autocratic principal or teacher should be aware of the possible reactions to that particular style. Fear — physical fear, fear of losing a job, ridicule — may keep followers in line. Somewhere, however, a reaction is building which may come out in many different ways — vandalism, non-co-operation, deliberate misunderstanding, disorder when authority is absent. In classrooms, where safety is important, such a situation means that pupils can be left alone only at great risk. Laissez-faire leadership is probably not common in classrooms. But it can occur indirectly when teachers are ill-prepared, tired, ill, or not interested in what they are doing. The principal must make sure this does not happen. Fellow staff-members can also lend a hand. Laissez-faire principals are not common, but some who are retiring soon or who perhaps feel inadequate or would sooner take it easy are apt to withdraw in this manner. If this goes on too long, the staff sometimes conducts a polite "mutiny."

Democratic leadership in a school does not mean "one person-one vote." Political democracy is taken into account when deciding internal arrangements and group structures, but the group decides neither the leader or the task. The group may take part in the decision, but the responsibility belongs to the leader. This style can, at least in principle, be seen in a school setting. The principal is appointed by the board of education on the advice of the appropriate supervisory officer(s) or of selection committees.

Various acts, regulations and curriculum guidelines set out the general aim of a school; therefore, the individual school actually does not have much flexibility. The implementation of these aims, however, is another matter. Herein lies the chance of using a "democratic" leadership style. The principal's leadership determines how staff meetings are conducted: the methods of running meetings, who contributes, who conducts the meeting, how decisions are arrived at.

In the classroom, the approach must be somewhat more subtle. The subject matter and the age of pupils can alter leadership styles so much. The lesson of the hobby clubs are significant for teachers who want to establish a warm, trusting climate in the classroom. One teacher put it this way—"This is a democracy, with me firmly in charge." Commenting on these styles, Newnham and Nease (1970) suggest that a laissez-faire situation may even occur when principals abrogate their authority because they have an "erroneous view of democratic administration." Indeed, such principals allow their staffs to make decisions on "even the most trifling item concerning the administration of the school." The same authors suggest a spectrum of administration as applied to the principal in a school.

Figure 3.1 The Administration Spectrum

Laissez-faire	Democratic	Authoritarian
The principals leave all decision-making in the hands of staff members, causing "dangling" decisions.	The principals, without giving up any authority and legal responsibility, share some decision-making with their staff members.	The principals, relying on their legal positions in the hierarchy, make all decisions unilaterally.

(Newnham and Nease, 1970)

3.2 More Recent Developments

Since the Second World War, research into leadership has focussed on analysis of what leaders actually do as well as the relations between the leader and followers. Owens (1981) views leadership as a process: "a process through which others are influenced to achieve goals in a specific situation. Thus, the important elements of leadership are (1) the behaviour of the leader, (2) the behaviour of the followers and (3) the environment of the situation."

According to the literature on leadership, two dimensions emerge: a concern about people in the organization and their needs (back-slapping and baby-kissing); a concern for the needs of the organization (keeping the paper-work moving). The latter pre-supposes the systems approach to the organization insofar as it is agreeable to think of organizations possessing needs; some researchers disagree, for the needs of the people who make up the organization are more important. Regardless of this interpretative viewpoint, the studies in leadership behaviour to which we shall refer are deeply rooted in the systems metaphor.

The most useful place to begin the study of leadership behaviour as applied to schools is the Ohio State University Studies in Leadership, reported by Halpin (1966). As a basis, Stogdill and his associates developed a set of twelve dimensions of leadership. Further research resulted in the development of the Leader Behaviour Description Questionnaire (LBDQ). The LBDQ was first developed by John Hemphill and Alvin Coons (see Halpin, 1966), but has since undergone many refinements. This particular instrument identified two primary dimensions:

Initiating structure—the delineation of the relationships between the leader and the members of the group and the establishment of ways of getting the job done.

Consideration—behaviour indicating friendship, trust and warmth between the leader and members of the group.

3.3 Measuring Leadership

Halpin (1966) cautions that this questionnaire measures the leader's behaviour in a specified situation "but does not purport to measure an intrinsic capacity for leadership." The dimensions do not necessarily constitute *the* only criterion of effective leadership. "However, they probably do represent *a* criterion that should be taken into account in evaluating leadership skills." The LBDQ-Form XIII (a refined version of Form I) encompasses twelve sub-scales, covering the range of leader behaviours. It includes factors considered to be significant in leadership. The instrument measures the frequency with which administrators exhibit each "leader behaviour" to their staff. The sub-scales are described in the Manual (Stogdill, 1963), but a brief summary of each follows:

(1) *System-Oriented*
   - production emphasis: actively promotes increased output
   - initiation of structure: clearly defines leader's role and those of followers
   - representation: acts as the representative of the group (leader and followers)
   - role assumption: willingly undertakes the task of leadership
   - persuasion: persuades others with effective arguments; has strong convictions
   - superior orientation: maintains good relations with superiors; seeks higher status

(2) *Person-Oriented*
   - tolerance of freedom: encourages initiative among the staff
   - tolerance of uncertainty: tolerates uncertainty with equanimity
   - consideration: is concerned about the comfort and well-being of the followers
   - demand reconciliation: reconciles conflicting demands and restores order to chaos
   - predictive accuracy: has foresight and predicts outcomes with accuracy
   - integration: maintains a closely-knit organization and resolves conflicts between members

The analysis of the twelve parts into the two dimensions noted above was the result of studies by Alan Brown (1967). System-orientation measures behaviour which deals with the needs of the organization as a system; systems-oriented individuals are interested in exercising a managerial style of leadership which leads to productive output. Person-orientation measures that behaviour which deals with the needs of staff members as persons; person-oriented individuals tend to have a high concern for the well-being, status and contributions of followers.

But who is an effective leader? Using the two dimensions above and constructing a two-by-two matrix, we find four possible combinations:

Figure 3.2   Leadership Styles Using LBDQ Dimensions

Quadrant II Low Consideration High Initiating Structure	Quadrant I High Consideration High Initiating Structure
Quadrant III Low Consideration Low Initiating Structure	Quadrant IV High Consideration Low Initiating Structure

The LBDQ includes one hundred statements. The respondent (a "follower") marks each according to how often the leader seems to act in each case. For example, statement No. 1 is: "He acts as the spokesman of the group" to which the respondent replies by circling the appropriate letter, A = always, B = often, C = occasionally, D = seldom, E = never. The composite scores are then computed, weighted and converted with the two-dimensional profile.

In the matrix presented in Fig. 3-2, the leadership style in Quadrant I represents those who are high on both dimensions; they would appear to be most effective in this case. Brown (1967), however, found that teachers were prepared to consider principals to be "good" principals if they scored highly on one of the two dimensions and at least "average" on the other. Quadrant III represents leaders who are low in both dimensions; these tend to be ineffective. As was noted above, they would be seen as relatively ineffective, but nevertheless exhibiting some behaviour that staff can note.

3.4   Fiedler's Contingency Model

There are other studies of leadership, but this book shall discuss only Fiedler's Contingency Theory of Leadership. This model was developed in other fields, but has been tested in school situations. Fiedler (1967) points out that the person-oriented leader and the task-oriented leader are equally effective. His contingency model is based upon two factors: individual needs and the leadership style. The situation does affect behaviour, whereas a person's prior intentions turn out to be less important in the event. Fiedler (1967) further states that "important leadership behaviours of the same individual differ from situation to situation, while the need-structure which motivates these behaviours may be seen as constant." Fiedler also classified leaders as being either task-oriented or human relation-oriented. The former achieve satisfaction from getting the job done, the latter from establishing successful interpersonal relations.

To determine the style of leadership, Fiedler developed a "least-Preferred Co-Worker Scale." The persons tested describes the actions of the persons they worked with least well. Task-oriented leaders (who responded in harsher terms about their co-workers) were most effective in situations of high or low control, whereas the relation-oriented leaders were most effective in control situations between these two. Leaders will be most effective when they operate in situations that are favorable to their individual styles. In addition,

> the group's effectiveness is contingent on the interaction between two variables: (1) the motivational system of the leader — his style in relating to his group and (2) the favorableness of the group situation — the degree to which the situation allows the leader to control his group (Roe and Drake, 1980).

In a situation of high control, no further consideration is necessary; the support is already there. In the low-control situation, it takes a real effort to clean up the mess and a task-oriented style is called for. In the middle case, it is possible to operate by building good relationships; these efforts should result in more effective leadership. But Fiedler (1967) concluded that a person's leadership style was difficult to change because it reflected one's aspirations.

How does Fiedler's model apply to the school? A highly structured task, like preparing the time-table for a staff with good relations, a strong principal, and a favorable situation, calls for a task-oriented style. The staff members trust the principal's judgement and are content to have the job done. A not-so-strong principal, however, faced with a relatively unstructured task (for example, what should be done with the reading problem in the junior division?), in a favorable situation, will use a human relations-oriented style to garner support.

But the principal's power has been affected by pressure from higher up in the hierarchy, and from teachers' federations, especially by collective bargaining. The principal's diminishing power is possibly causing a tilt towards a relations-oriented style. The increase in programs and widening in the backgrounds of the clients have also led to more diffuse problems. Drugs, discipline, socio-economic factors, and changing attitudes are as easy to deal with as diploma requirements or curriculum guidelines. Gilbert *et al.* (1977) found that educational leaders believed they knew how to cope with the mechanical side of the job but lacked the necessary interpersonal skills.

3.5 The Principal—Leadership in Practice

Principals must work with many different people. Like a lion tamer in the ring with eight large cats, they must have eyes for them all, ears for them all, concern for them all.

What kind of people become principals? If they have anything in common, they are interested in people: how they react, behave, and learn. In other respects, they are different. They are not all dynamic, nor smart, nor industrious. They are not all well educated. Most importantly, they have different goals.

Principals begin by first becoming teachers, one hopes, good ones. Then, as they accomplish what they had set out to do, they look for other things. If they lean towards working with people, they seek an administrative position.

It is easier to explain who should become a principal than to describe those who do so. Principals should love children and young people and want to help them. Principals should be good organizers, good fighters, good mediators. They should be honest. They should be good communicators and hard workers.

It takes a bit of luck to get this position. The academic requirements are reasonable. Because the courses are often offered at night or summer school, it is not necessary to give up teaching to take them. It is getting somewhat more difficult to get promoted: one is now expected to have most of a master's degree, and the appointments are fewer and the selection committees more political than they used to be.

The on-the-job training available to teachers varies from school to school and from board to board. In some areas, teachers get experience by teaching a class or two less and spending that time in the school office doing administrative work. In other areas, teachers' federations have negotiated contracts that prohibit taking teachers out of the classroom because the rest of the staff must then take larger classes. Here the interested teacher must get the in-service training by giving up unassigned time or working before or after school. It is surprising that school boards have not recognized the value of this on-the-job training and that they have been so willing to give up such items in contract negotiations.

Teachers, federations and boards should recognize the benefits of the best training possible. Courses can only teach so much; apprenticeships in the schools should be an additional requirement.

Much of the principal's job is prescribed by the acts or the regulations. Each board of education has books of policies and operating procedures that define operating. Contracts between the board and the federation further prescribe salaries and working conditions for teachers. These may limit the ways a principal can deploy staff and operate programs. Local school policies and operating procedures are set out in handbooks issued to staff and students and, in secondary schools, in documents like the calendars of courses. Some principals help prepare these. The ministries of education also issue guidelines, memos, and documents to define programs and to remind principals and staff of special events. But all these rules and regulations and guidelines are not enough to define completely the role of the principal.

The principal's job has changed. It is much more legalistic than it used to be, with more rules and more conflicts. There is more paper pushing and central control. The boards seem to have less faith in the principal; the students and staff show less respect.

What then is the role of the principal? One definition states that "a leader must find out which way the herd is going and then get around in front." But it is more than that. Principals must not forget that education is a people-business.

They must ensure that the school gives every student a fair chance to succeed and prepare the student for a changing world. There must be discipline for those who cannot discipline themselves. The rules must be fairly administered.

Principals must set an example for the staff, with standards of dress and deportment and language, and hard work. They must encourage the staff and protect them from unfair criticism. It is their duty to evaluate the staff, honestly and fairly. They must keep the staff informed, especially of board and ministry policies as they affect the staff and the school. Principals must give the staff fair opportunities for professional development and advancement.

Principals must delegate responsibility well. Vice-principals have real areas of authority and need freedom to operate. Other senior members of the staff must be treated with respect, not constantly subject to veto by the principal. Principals must accept the fact that appeal is always possible but they must also feel they will be supported if they have acted in a sensible and reasonable manner.

Other important positions include those of department head and grade chairman. The principal should treat these people as branch managers and as a school cabinet, give them support and let them set policy.

Under the best conditions, they are in control of their own areas of responsibility and whenever possible are involved in selecting staff. They are in charge of programs and have the freedom to operate within the limits of that budget. With the proper position, they are a strong force in interpreting policies to the rest of the staff.

The elementary school often lacks this group, at least in an official and paid way. If this is so, the wise principal identifies leaders, perhaps according to educational divisions, seniority and experience, or the needs of the moment. These leaders act as an unofficial cabinet and sounding board and help set and carry out policy.

The entire staff can be used for the good of the school. The team structure proposed above or a judicious use of committees gives those interested a chance to find out how policies are set and best administered. Another real benefit comes in the staff member finding that it is not easy to administer. Just as letting students teach helps them to understand what a teacher's life is like, so allowing staff to become involved in the administration helps them to understand why things are done the way they are. They also become more supportive.

Principals must also get involved in public relations. It is important to make sure that the public not have any misconceptions about the school. This applies to parents, to board officials, to the community. The principal must be the voice of the school.

Principals should participate in the various principals' organizations, in their professional development programs and their business functions. Too often policies are set by those too far removed from the school. Principals are the ambassadors who must carry the messages to the right places and to the right people.

3.6   Democratic Leadership in Action—
The Principal and Decision-Making

As in so many other things the principal does, what counts is not so much what is done as what is perceived to be done. Principals must be seen to be firm yet kind, decisive yet willing to listen. They must be strong leaders yet be of the people.

Involvement has its disadvantages. Principals should not allow a vote on anything at a staff meeting which they are not prepared to accept. If the principals first allow a vote, but then veto an unfavourable decision, there is trouble. Many principals like to listen to suggestions and then make the decision alone. This also causes problems. If the principals decide against most suggestions, then they are seen as dictatorial and even dishonest. They must be careful. If they are sure they know what must be done, then perhaps they should not consult at all. It would be better just to explain what must be done and why. Some of the staff will complain, but there always will be some who complain. At least, the principals will not seem just to go through the motions of consulting.

Many cases obviously do not have just one right answer. Principals should consult others as often as possible and do so in a positive way. They should listen carefully to others to find the most satisfying alternatives for the most people. There may be draw-backs no matter what is done, but having commitment from the group will help to carry the matter forward.

There is nothing wrong in admitting that one is not sure. If the problem has no easy solution, then asking for advice of those one trusts is a good idea. Many department heads and senior teachers are just as experienced as the principal. Their expertise should not remain untapped.

Unfortunately, principals may not always feel comfortable in consulting the superintendents. Perhaps the superintendents are not as experienced as the principals. Nevertheless, the superintendents can help, by giving advice, testing out a plan, providing resources and support. Often, it is a simple matter of keeping the superintendent informed in case the superintendent has to look at the whole mess in the future.

The principal who knows the board policies and implements the good ones in place for that school does not have to repeat the same decisions over and over. For example, sometimes parents want to take students out of school for special holiday trips at inconvenient times. The principals cannot be making that decision every time. A school policy, supported by the board, should deal with this. Of course, the parents may not always agree, but policies give some stability to the school. Teachers can predict the solutions in many straight-forward cases, and the staff are assured they will be supported when they implement policy.

Let us examine the above case one step further. The parent wants to take the student out at examination time. Does the student need to miss the whole day? Perhaps a few hours are enough. One possible solution is the following: the student will write the examination at 7 a.m. in a special room supervised by someone in the office; the parent will pick the student up right at that room and will guarantee the student will not talk to other students about the examination. Thus, the principal has supported the policy and accommodated people.

In successful schools, senior staff members are involved in preparing policy. The principals listen carefully, then write the policy and give it

back to them to review. They accept suggested improvements, then final-
ize the policy and present it to the staff as having senior staff support.
When there are questions, the principals turn to the senior staff: "Did we
consider that point? Why did we do that?" or "I think we did that
because..." or "That's a good idea. We didn't think of that. Why don't
we incorporate that into the policy? All in favour? Thank you for the
good idea."

In somewhat the same way, policies must also be reviewed from time
to time. Out-of-date policy can cause all kinds of trouble.

Decision-making where students take part must be handled delicately.
Principals want to give them good direction. On the other hand, they also
want the students to feel involved; and youngsters will not learn to make
decisions if they can never make any. Student government members need
some power to make decisions in certain areas; they will work much
harder when they think it is their idea. But they still need guidance, to
prevent serious or costly mistakes.

Involvement encourages hard work and support. Even the best policies
and best decisions will fail without support.

Not all decisions should be made quickly. Often, the principals must
pause and think a bit. In difficult cases, principals should not be afraid to
say they want to think about it overnight and will get back tomorrow or,
perhaps the principals will consult the heads or senior staff: "I think we
will likely do this, but I want to consult with the senior staff before we
go ahead." Perhaps the decision is up to the vice-principal. Principals
should not take over what has been delegated to staff or even students.
They should simply inform the person asking for a ruling to whom it
would be proper to go. Only if the matters may come back on appeal
should the principals become involved.

Appeals can be a bit tricky. All parties should attend the hearing. First,
the principal listens to the complaint and the reasons for the decision,
then questions everyone and asks for alternatives. If the persons who
made a mistake now realize it, they can now suggest the correction rather
than wait for the principal to impose it. Is there a reasonable compromise
or correction? Would more research help? Perhaps the ideal solution is
just not possible.

4 Innovation

4   Innovation

4.1   Discussion of Terms

Hoyle (1972) suggests that "change" is a generic term which includes innovation, reform, renewal or development. "Change" often means only that some idea, object or practice has altered whereas "innovation" has overtones of deliberate planning (Huberman, 1973). The distinction is not always followed, for example, "planned change" and "unplanned change." Hoyle (1972) suggests "innovation" can mean either a specific act or a process.

Here we shall use "change" as a generic term, "innovation" to describe a new idea, object or practice, and "implementation" the result of a change. In addition, there is an important distinction to be made between "innovative" and "progressive." Using Huberman's (1973) definition, an "innovative program" employs "the creative selection, organization and utilization of human and material resources in new and unique ways which will result in the attainment of a higher level of achievement for the desired goals and objectives."

"Progressivism" grows out of Dewey's philosophy; it emphasizes freedom, individual desires, immediate goals, pupil-initiative, pragmatism and process (Encyclopedia of Modern Education). Changes that lead in this direction may be classified as "progressive." Changes can be innovative without necessarily being progressive.

The CERI (1973) volume on struggles for innovation suggests that innovative schools are characterized by:

- New decision-making structures
- Openness towards the outside world
- Development, rather than invention, of innovations within the school

— The replacement by environmental (for example, parental) control of state-imposed external controls

— "Readiness" of the total school culture towards innovation

The CERI studies suggest that fewer external constraints do not necessarily mean more freedom for a school. In fact, external constraints often provide a shelter behind which a school may experiment, especially if the constraints reflect expectations in society or a description of the way we wish schools to behave. Leadership is important here, affecting the selection, recruitment and promotion of staff.

Little is known of the organizational receptiveness to innovation. Burns and Stalker (1961) suggest that if members of an organization have made many changes, they are likely to make even more. Greiner (1967) writes that this occurs because of outside pressure and internal tension.

Much of the literature describes innovative schools by listing practices. Thomas (1975) reports that the most widely used method of ranking relative innovativeness is the time-adoption scale. He warns that it has a major weakness: it includes only innovations developed elsewhere and imported into the schools; it does not recognize internal generation of innovation. And he cautions that the findings indicate only frequency and time of adoption. They tell us little or nothing about the organizational structure, changed interpersonal relations or success.

4.2 Studies of Adoption and Diffusion of Innovations in Schools

Rogers (1962), and Rogers and Shoemaker (1971) examined many adoption and diffusion studies. Rogers (1962) reviewed more than 500 studies, while Rogers and Shoemaker (1971) list approximately 1200 empirical and over 300 non-empirical diffusion research publications. In general, the latter studies deal with simple innovations (techniques or devices) among individuals (farmers, doctors, for example). Studies in education have been concerned primarily with innovation in schools and school systems. Rogers' model of adoption was developed from these studies. Although it has been used to analyze successful innovations into schools (Eichholz and Rogers, 1964; Miles, 1964; Carlson, 1965; Owens, 1970), it is nevertheless based on innovations by individuals. Rogers also studies how the social structure of a system affects change, and vice versa. He developed a series of propositions, including the following:

— Power elites act as gatekeepers to prevent restructuring innovations from entering a social system. They favour functioning innovations that do not immediately threaten to change the system's structure.

- Top-down change in a system initiated by the power-elites is more likely to succeed than a bottom-up change.
- Bottom-up change causes more conflict than top-down change.

These propositions imply a clear "we-they" conflict.

4.3 Innovation and Organizational Variables

This deficiency leads us to a consideration of innovation in terms of organizational variables. Gross *et al.* (1971) writes that most change is imposed from above in an organization. Therefore, the structure is more significant than the people in determining innovation. Superordinates must prepare the way for it. In another model, the individual brings about innovation. In Carlson's (1965) adoption study, the superordinates, not their subordinates, make changes.

Writing on curriculum change, Hoyle introduces three other dimensions: organizational analysis, curriculum change, and the role of the teacher. He uses the metaphor of organizational health (Miles, 1965), with the concept of "tissue-rejection" to describe the organization's natural tendency to reject. He suggests (1972) that it is organizational innovation that should be dealt with first so that process innovation will then fit more easily.

House is another author who would re-structure educational organization to encourage innovation tendencies. He focusses on diffusion, but he relates it to organizations by categorizing those within in terms of susceptibility to change. The top administrators are more closely involved in change because teachers are too busy in the classroom to make the necessary external contacts. He sees a lack of interest at the lowest level in the hierarchy, and writes that teachers do not want to take chances on innovation unless they are dissatisfied.

4.4 Dissemination and Utilization

The literature on dissemination and utilization is extensive. A major work is that of Havelock's whose models (1969) are important in the study of how the user learns about, and adopts a specific innovation. In developing his models, Havelock writes that there are few case-studies, especially about new organizational forms. He acknowledges his debt to Rogers (1962). Although he notes that Rogers' work lacks educational sources, it does rely heavily on numerical correlations about individuals, and little organizational change.

His basic model includes three categories: Research, Development and Diffusion; Social-Interaction; and Problem-Solving. None is representative or comprehensive. His "linkage" model states that senders and receivers interact and try to appreciate each other's needs. These relationships "can become channels for rapid, effective and efficient transfer of information." Such a proposition seems to be speculation and is too idealistic. Havelock relies too much on the resource person (change agent) and relationships.

Havelock suggests the role of government is to support and coordinate linkage activities to make the system more effective. He assumes the users rely on this support. This is consistent with the overtones of the paternalistic, external consultant found throughout his writing.

Nevertheless, Havelock's three categories led to three popular models. It is necessary to examine them in view of the above criticism. We will look at each of his models separately, to adopt his "package" as a framework for examining innovation.

The Research, Development and Diffusion Model. The steps in the model are more easily accomplished when the adoption system is centralized. The model assumes that an innovation will be adopted by all in an organization. This is not always the case; it depends on the environment and the values of the users.

The model is excessively idealistic and research-oriented. According to Fullan (1972), much of the suggested change is transmitted on a "relatively universalistic basis" and the values and goals of users do not directly influence the process. Neither Fullan nor Havelock discusses anything but a universalistic set of management goals with respect to innovation. Fullan does recommend a climate that encourages discussion on educational choices involving all constituencies — students, parents, teachers, administrators.

Social Interaction Model (SIM). Havelock's model has five steps: Awareness, Interest, Evaluation, Trial and Adoption. The model relies on communication from person to person and from system to system, somewhat like a communicable disease.

Common criticism of this model is that it appears to work best for individual adopters, whereas in education the school is the adopting unit. The model also assumes a centrally-generated, unitary pre-disposition. Innovation can take place in relative isolation as long as the organization structure accommodates it; in this case, leadership is important. Isolation also permits conflicting goals, again as long as some structure acts as a control. Fullan (1972) was troubled by the conflict caused by some of the permissive innovation ("progressivism"), which others view as disastrous — hence his suggestion of a climate which permits discussion.

Havelock's SIM and many of its critics do not pay enough attention to organizational factors. Havelock does refer to theoretical work on the different ways information is transmitted. His model is based on a scientific model developed by Bhola (1965).

Figure 4.1   The Research, Development and Diffusion Model

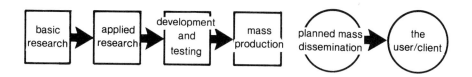

Figure 4.2   The Social Interaction Model

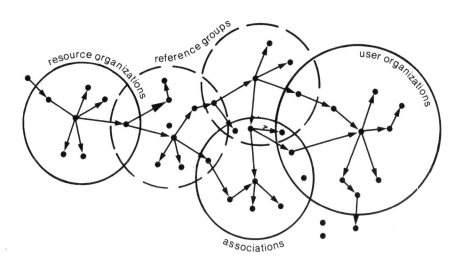

Problem Solving Model (PSM). Here the user is the starting point. Havelock suggests the outside helpers—the agents of change—frequently take a major role; the danger is that they may dominate the process completely. In Havelock's view, the outside expert's role is to convey essential information to the user. There is the risk that the user will rely on this source and never learn to initiate changes himself. This is as close as Havelock comes to discussing the autonomy or professionality that may be significant in organizational change. The use of outside consultants and help is a theme that can be seen throughout Havelock's work. He also states that the PSM might well be the only model of utilization, but this is perhaps too great a claim.

Figure 4.4   Problem Solving Model

The model assumes that the innovation satisfies the needs of the users.

Initial disturbance (pressure from
inside or outside, crisis, etc.)

Satisfaction that problem is   Feeling of need and decision to
solved or dissatisfaction re-   do something about the need
sulting in repeat of cycle

Application of a possible solu-   Diagnosis of need as a problem
tion to the need

Search for solutions

In general, Havelock's models have become prescriptive as they dominate the literature. The PSM makes a strong argument, for example, about the benefits of using agents of change. It is only a short step from recommending that some do it to claiming that all should. Although Havelock notes the "needs reduction cycle" could apply to a process within an organization, he clearly states that outside agents are more effective. Discussing the social interaction model, he notes that there is some disagreement with his system's view of society where "each part is orchestrated toward a common system output." This is in the nature of a note in passing, however, and he does not pursue the idea.

4.5   Strategies of Change

Strategies for implementing change were analysed and described by Chinn and Benne (1969), who developed a prominent model. It consists of three types:

Rational-empirical. It assumes that people are reasonable and once they understand the efficacy of an innovation they will adopt it. Of course, different people will have different opinions.

Power-coercive. Those less powerful simply follow the lead or instructions of one more powerful. The use of legal and administrative power is common. Governments, schools, and teachers use it.

Figure 4.5 Problem-solving Model (with external change agent)

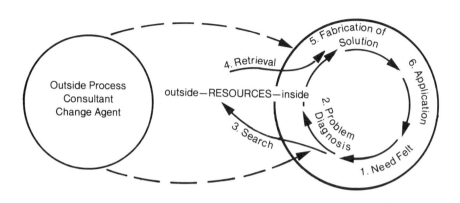

Normative—re-educative. Innovations are adopted when people are re-educated to change their values, attitudes and relationships. This involves manipulation. If outsiders (for example, change agents) are brought in to do the re-educating, they may cause problems by upsetting relationships.

The authors admit that these divisions are arbitrary and seldom found in their pure forms. Their application may vary in different circumstances. Unfortunately, they cannot be relied upon in a general way. For example, bringing about change depends on how centralized is the control of a large system. Nevertheless, the concepts do explain organizational change although they all involve external persuasion.

Hoyle (1970, 1971b) suggests that principals may be change agents. How do they use their authority and power? If they use their power to overcome resistance, they do not fit Rogers' (1962) definition of the change agent as a "local low level bureaucrat whose purpose is to inject a cosmopolite influence to innovate into a client social system." The power-coercive strategy is possible. With the changing role of the principal in recent times, it is now more necessary to rely on the rational-empirical or normative-re-educative strategies. This duality, of course, is too simple: the principal may be able to confuse power and authority by arranging the structure so that all parties in the organization believe they are attaining their goals simultaneously.

4.6   Correlates of Innovation

Most studies of change are concerned with the intrinsic characteristics of innovations, innovators and adopting units.

Intrinsic Characteristics of Innovations. Miles (1964b) is a widely-cited
authority. He writes that properties of an innovation — the cost, technological factors, associated materials, difficulty of implementation, and
suitability — all affect its adoption. Rogers' (1962) list of factors influencing adoption dealt solely with the perceptions of adopters to
specific innovations. He did not refer to the "receptiveness" of the organization.

Rogers' list also includes relative advantage, compatibility with the
adopting system, complexity, divisibility of the innovation, and ease of
explanation.

Compatibility with the system raises the question of values. Neither
Rogers nor Miles goes any further than regarding it as an internal characteristic which invariably hinders acceptance and diffusion of externally
imposed values.

Characteristics of Innovators. A more widespread approach to the study
of adoption includes characteristics of "adopting units," ranging from
communities and schools to principals and teachers. Such studies report
that innovators:
  − possess high intelligence (Miles, 1964b; Havelock, 1970)
  − travel widely or are cosmopolitan (Rogers, 1965; Havelock, 1970)
  − rely on outside sources for ideas (Woods, 1967; Havelock, 1970)
  − are rebellious (Miles, 1964b; Woods, 1967)
  − are mavericks (Miles, 1964b; Rogers, 1965; Havelock, 1970)
  − are confident (Miles, 1964b; Lippitt, 1967).

Other qualities include commitment to the profession (Lippitt,
1967); high social status (Rogers, 1965); ambition (Woods, 1967);
strength (Miles, 1964b); and the exercise of opinion leadership
(Rogers, 1965). These are all personal qualities. Most of the literature
looks at personal adoption rather than organizational structure, goals or
attitudes.

Environmental Factors and Adopting Units. Most studies of environmental factors are American. They look at school boards and their location, or the size of schools and school districts. Thomas (1975) lists
studies of economic factors, including salaries and facilities, and the
wealth of schools and school districts.

4.7   Organizational Health

The literature of innovation has not paid much attention to the form of the organization. Some authors, Smith and Keith (1971) for example, suggest that educational change requires three components:
- organizational structures and attitudes among higher authorities to encourage innovation
- tolerance to change on the part of the users
- skills of users to perform new roles.

Such a list leads to an examination of groups, changing attitudes, intentions, and skills. For example, in an examination of organizations, Argyris (1957) writes that a bureaucracy creates passivity, submissiveness and dependency among individual workers.

A more widespread term, however, is Miles' (1965) "organizational health." He uses a biological systems analogy, including "clear organization goals", "adequacy of communication", "equalization of influence upwards and downwards." He also includes systems' maintenance needs (morale, cohesiveness) and other dimensions that deal with change. Miles states that healthy systems invent new procedures, create new goals and grow, rather than remain routinized and standard.

Clark (1970), however, suggests that organizational health is present when two tendencies, change and stability, co-exist; it is to management's advantage to consider the needs of individuals in the organization. Although he is writing of an industrial organization, his suggestions raise the question of progressive and traditional values and norms. It may be possible to arrange an organizational structure based on Clark's concept, but including receptiveness to innovation. Such a structure could meet the concerns of Fullan (1972), who believes that if they want change, administrators must listen to teachers. Fullan concludes that in the past fifteen years very little significant change has taken place, despite many attempts; the users have had little influence on the changes; and the values or goals of users have not influenced the process.

The goals and values of clients have also been neglected, even at the user level, except perhaps when the schools are being evaluated (Smith and Keith, 1971).

If they conflict with the official mandate for the school, the goals and values of the clients and community may have a different effect upon innovation.

4.8   Implementation

In the past decade, there has been more attention on implementation, that is, how innovations are institutionalized for the consumers.

Fullan (1982) examines the actions of a "district administrator," a superintendent of some kind. Whereas many innovations have been sponsored at this level, the ministries of education have also initiated some major changes, albeit after some urging, for example, the credit diploma, and provisions for special education. We shall look at another approach to implementation by Berman and McLaughlin (1976). They investigated the phenomenon of unsuccessful innovations. The study was set up because the U.S. Office of Education was concerned about the failures of federally-funded special programs. Berman and McLaughlin (1976) developed a model which described the innovative process. It identified three steps: initiation, implementation, and incorporation. The model is useful in analysing changes in schools. Gilbert (1982) described it as follows:

> They identified in the initial stage two types — *opportunities* and *problem-solving.* . . . It was noted that projects imported from outside usually failed to gather support or to generate staff involvement. In the *implementation* stage, Berman and McLaughlin observed three kinds of interaction between projects and settings. They were (1) mutual adaptation; adaptation of both the project design and the institutional setting; (2) non-implementation, i.e., no adaptation or change and (3) cooptation; adaptation of the project to the indifference and resistance of participants but no change by the participants themselves.

By comparing each step in the implementation with each stage in the initiation, they found that adaptation occurred only if people were committed to it. They identified the "scope of change," defined as follows:
— closeness to central objectives of the district
— amount of change required
— congruency with goals and practices of the district
— complexity.
According to Berman and McLaughlin (1976), an innovation needs the wholehearted support of the school for it to succeed. Unless the goals and values associated with a change suit those of the potential adopters, success is unlikely, or else the innovation is adopted superficially.

The approach to the study of innovation has changed. Once studies focussed on how different personalities interact. This study, among many others, turns towards values, attitudes and goals both within the adopting unit and in its environment. Studies such as Gross *et al.* (1971) and Smith and Keith (1971) demonstrate that the presence of certain logistical standards is simply not enough to secure the success of a change.

For a description of the relationships between school, the teacher, the principal and the environment on one hand and change on the other, Fullan's book *The Meaning of Educational Change* provides up-to-date information: it is a catalogue of the change processes and also contains many insightful analyses.

Principals and teachers, the professional staff of a school, should be the prime movers in change. If innovations are to be imposed from above, then the communication with the users should be complete. The faculties and colleges of education must teach their graduates about change; school boards and professional organizations must encourage practising teachers to take part in educational reform, based upon sound principles. Then, perhaps, the school, as the centre of education, can take its rightful place in the sun.

5 Organizational Climate

5   Organizational Climate

5.1   Climate and Morale

People do not work merely for the extrinsic rewards available; they also seek a sense of belonging to a group and being expected to measure up to its standards and norms. Indeed, this feeling applies to work groups, as well as a much larger population. School spirit, societies, university alumni associations, and the like are all manifestations of it. Many, however, try to establish the converse; that is, a "school spirit" organization will produce good morale. It does not always work.

According to a concept of morale, hierarchical management structures are no longer the only determinant of success; managers and administrators must take into account also the interpersonal dynamics of groups involved within the organization. To guide organizations effectively one must understand the principles of group morale. This is important since the recent increased emphasis on participation in decision-making. Many principals have not yet come to terms with this approach. But the role of management is changing in general and the participation by teachers is becoming more institutionalized. The law does set limits, of course. (These were noted in Chapter 3 in the discussion of leadership.) In recent years such changes have affected supervision in schools; for example, the provincial inspector became a program consultant.

How can one quantify the concept of morale? The concept may be described as "organizational climate." Forehand (1963) defines this as "a set of organizational properties which may influence the behaviour of individuals in organizations, e.g., the feeling of a school." The instrument most widely used to collect and measure data on school climates is the Organizational Climate Description Questionnaire (OCDQ), developed by Halpin and Croft (1963). They describe climate in the following terms:

> Anyone who visits more than a few schools notes quickly how schools differ from each other in their 'feel'.... As one moved to other schools, one finds that each appears to have a "personality" of its own. It is this personality we describe as the "Organizational Climate" of the school. Analogously, personality is to the individual what Organizational Climate is to the organization.

Halpin explains that the climates in the OCDQ were devised or "invented" and draws attention to the danger of attempting to fit the phenomena to the definition. Nevertheless, the questionnaire is widely used to measure climate and establish correlation studies.

The OCDQ was developed by analysing the "climates" of seventy-one elementary schools in six different regions of the United States, using responses of 1151 teachers. It consists of sixty-four items, assigned to eight different sub-tests. Four of these pertain to characteristics of teachers as a group, four to characteristics of the principal as leader. The eight dimensions of organizational climate are described in detail in Halpin and Croft (1963). Halpin and Croft identified a set of six organizational climates from these eight sub-tests, based upon the content. They are briefly described here. Full details are found in Halpin (1966).

- *The Open Climate* is a situation where members work well together, and find the principal's policies let them get on with the job.
- *The Autonomous Climate* is one where the principal lets teachers find ways to satisfy their social needs. The principal remains relatively aloof, is considerate, and works hard.
- *The Controlled Climate* emphasizes achievement, with little time for social needs or friendly relations. Nevertheless, morale is high. Teachers get on with the job and expect direction. Social isolation is common.
- *The Familiar Climate* focusses on the satisfaction of social needs rather than task-achievement.
- In *the Paternal Climate* teachers do not work well together. The principal does most of the paper work and receives little help from the teachers. The principal is always checking up on staff.
- *The Closed Climate* is characterized by low satisfaction in both task-achievement and social needs. The principal emphasizes production but does not set a good example.

Climates are based upon staff perceptions; a climate is "open" if the staff members believe it to be. Halpin took this stand. It would be a mistake, however, to rely entirely upon mathematical models when evidence is also available by recording individual perceptions.

In conclusion, it is possible that the sub-scales of the OCDQ are more significant in understanding the school than are the climates developed from them. And the absence of suitable norms is often a deficiency in using the OCDQ.

5.2   The Effect of Climate on Innovation

Carver and Sergiovanni (1969a) state that the OCDQ is not suited to large schools because of their complex nature. They also state that secondary schools by their nature tend to have closed climates. Halpin (1966), however, writes that the OCDQ is just as suitable for other kinds of schools as it is for elementary schools. Halpin and Croft (1963) state that the open climate encourages the most innovation; such organizations tend to be lively and move toward goals while satisfying the members of the organization. After further reflection, Halpin (1967) said that the relationship between climate and innovation is still unknown. Obviously, it is foolish to assume too much on the limited evidence available. Barnes (1967) suggests that autonomy does not flourish in closed climates; open climates emphasize technical expertise and subordinate authority. Halpin and Croft recommend the OCDQ as a measure of a school's "effectiveness". The evidence, however, does not clearly point to any predictable relationship between climates and cognitive learning.

A. Ross Thomas (1976) provides a most useful discussion of organizational climate in schools in a review of the literature in the *International Review of Education*. He discusses schools as organizations, the measurement of organizational climate (describing various instruments) and its relationship to innovation. He notes the prevalance of the OCDQ in the study of climate: "Organizational climate is a universal phenomenon. Despite its American origin, the OCDQ ... does appear to offer a basis for the cross-cultural study of school climate."

Thomas cautions, however, that "both scholar and practitioner must beware of confusing description with evaluation." It is a worthwhile warning, one that applies not only to climate.

Thomas' article concludes with a seven-page bibliography, a most useful list for the teacher or principal who would understand the concept better.

6   The Governance of Schools

6   The Governance of Schools

6.1   Governing Structures in Canada

The governance of schools in Canada is assigned to the federal and provincial jurisdictions under various sections of the Constitution Act, 1867 (formerly named the British North America Act, 1867.) Section 93 of the Constitution Act, 1867, states that:

In and for each Province the Legislature may exclusively make Laws in Relation to Education, subject and according to the following Provisions;

1. Nothing in any such Law shall prejudicially affect any Right or Privilege with respect to Denominational Schools which any Class of Persons have by Law in the Province at the Union;

2. All the Powers, Privileges and Duties at the Union by Law conferred and imposed in Upper Canada on the Separate Schools and School Trustees of the Queen's Roman Catholic Subjects shall be and the same are hereby extended to the Dissentient Schools of the Queen's Protestant and Roman Catholic Subjects in Quebec;

3. Where in any Province a System of Separate or Dissentient Schools exists by Law at the Union or is thereafter established by the Legislature of the Province, an Appeal shall lie to the Governor General in Council from any Act or Decision of any Provincial Authority affecting any Right or Privilege of the Protestant or Roman Catholic Minority of the Queen's Subjects in relation to Education;

4. In case of any such Provincial Law as from Time to Time seems to the Governor General in Council requisite for the due Execution of the Provisions of this Section is not made, or in case any Decision of the Governor General in Council on any Appeal under this Section is not duly executed by the proper Provincial Authority in that Behalf, then

and in every such Case, and as for only as the Circumstances of each
Case require, the Parliament of Canada may make remedial Laws for
the Due Execution of the Provisions of this Section and of any Decision of the Governor General in Council under this Section.

Thus, while the provinces have general authority over educational
affairs, they are subject to provisions affecting the rights of certain denominational groups.

The power of the provinces is restricted further. According to Section
91 of the Constitution Act, 1867, the Parliament of Canada has exclusive
jurisdiction over some other matters that include educational aspects:
Section 91 (7) Militia, Military and Naval Service and Defence; Section
91 (24) Indians and Lands reserved for Indians; and Section 91 (28) The
Establishment, Maintenance and Management of Penitentiaries.

Education in the Territories, of course, is a federal responsibility.

In effect, then, subject to the safeguards and exceptions mentioned
above, education is a provincial responsibility. The original Act applied
only to the four original provinces; as others joined, various agreements
were made which then governed each situation.

The matter of denominational or dissentient schools is explained quite
simply but in adequate detail in Giles (1978) *Educational Administration
in Canada.*

The organization of education varies from province to province. Some
common elements exist, however; for example, each has a minister of
education. The ministries or departments (the terminology varies) are
divided into sub-units under senior civil servants; the head in most
provinces is called the deputy-minister. Other government departments
also have a hand in the educational process; for example, natural resources
(forestry schools, mining schools), agriculture, fisheries, attorney-general
or social welfare (reformatories). In general, the provincial government
departments or ministries have control over supervision, certification of
teachers, curriculum and courses of study, selection of text books, and
regulations for schools, trustees, and teachers. The local school boards
within each province ensure accommodation, a sufficient number of
teachers, and the maintenance and repair of buildings. The central government has been the fountainhead of grants to local authorities. In earlier days, the grants were comparatively simple and based on numbers of
pupils, average daily attendance, and numbers of teachers. More recently,
political, social and educational pressures have led to a vastly more com-
plicated grant structure with respect to special education, transportation,
meals, language, and equalization. Civil servants now administer com-

plex regulations involving millions of dollars. For a time, examinations on a province-wide basis were eliminated; the current trend is towards reinstatement. The central authorities have expanded into other fields, including special education, libraries, educational media, computer services, vocational courses, correspondence courses, and even health and dental services.

The areas of responsibility change in response to demand and needs. Even such formerly rigid items as single sets of prescribed text books have given way to lists of authorized texts, from among which boards (not teachers, generally speaking) may choose.

The smaller local units of administration provide the schools and teachers. These school boards are generally elected; they raise money by a rate on property ("local taxes") and also receive funds from the central government. In recent years, more and more of the smaller boards, as well as the elementary and secondary school boards, have amalgamated. In the mid-19th century, for example, Ontario had approximately 4,500 boards; at present, there are about 200. Consolidation put an end to the "little red school house" (with its attendant myths). It has been replaced by larger schools, with their advantages: a wider curriculum, support services, and more specialist teachers. They also have certain disadvantages: increased hierarchy, transportation problems, and social complexities related to size. And the policies established to deal with rapid growth of the school system now must deal with declining enrolments.

6.11   The Governance of Education in Ontario

To study provincial governance of education, this book uses the example of Ontario.

In Ontario the main instrument is the *Education Act*, enacted by the Legislative Assembly and administered by the minister of education. Other laws under the jurisdiction of the minister include the Teaching Profession Act, the School Boards and Teachers Collective Negotiations Act, the Teachers' Superannuation Act, and the Ontario School Trustees' Council Act. The present minister of education is also minister of colleges and universities and has, in that capacity, jurisdiction over another group of acts including the Ministry of Colleges and Universities Act, the various acts governing the provincially assisted universities (for example, the Brock University Act), and other institutions (for example, the Ontario College of Art Act); related acts of interest (for example, the Sunnybrook Medical Centre Act); financial and properties acts; church-related acts (for example, the Assumption University Act); and acts relating to vocational education (for example, the Private Vocational Schools Act).

Acts administered by other ministries, like the Child Welfare Act and the Day Nurseries Act, impinge upon teachers and the care of children. The ministry of education is not the only agency that has responsibilities in this regard.

Under Part 1 of the Education Act, the minister of education has the authority over many important aspects of the educational system. These include matters affecting pupils and classrooms, including the issuing of diplomas and certificates, the prescribing of courses of study, the preparing of curriculum guidelines, and the approving of text books. Other powers of the minister include the certification of teachers, and the right to establish teachers' colleges and institutions for special education. Under Section 10 of the Act, the minister has the authority to make regulations about details concerned with the broad powers noted above. In particular, there are extensive regulations dealing with the daily operation of schools, summarized by Gilbert *et al.* (1984) as:

> school buildings, the school year, fees for various services, pupils' records, teachers' certificates, transportation, religious exercises and religious education, language of instruction, duties of pupils, the powers, duties and qualifications of teachers, principals and other personnel.

The school boards are left to provide the schools and teachers in their jurisdiction. There are many more duties which boards may assume and others which have been delegated (for example, supervision and evaluation).

There are different kinds of boards. Ontario, for example, had 171 boards in 1980. These included sixty-six boards of education, fifty combined Roman Catholic separate school boards of education, twenty-six public school boards of education, eight boards of education on crown land or Ontario Hydro property, eight Roman Catholic separate school boards, two Protestant separate school boards and one secondary school board of education.

Whether in counties, districts, cities or boroughs, boards of education operate public schools and secondary schools. Rates are levied on the property of public school supporters (whether owners or tenants) for the operation of elementary public schools, and on all taxpayers for the operation of secondary schools.

Combined Roman Catholic separate school boards operate separate elementary schools "from grades K-10." Taxes are collected from separate school supporters; they also pay taxes to the (public) board of education for the support of secondary schools. The other elementary boards (public or separate) exist in remote areas of the province where there are no secondary schools.

The ratepayers elect the trustees. Public school supporters elect members of a board of education, and separate school supporters elect members of separate school boards of education. Because the secondary schools are funded by all ratepayers, but operated by public boards, the separate school supporters also elect representatives on the public boards. Separate school supporters are Roman Catholics who have directed that their property taxes (either as owner or tenant) be used to support separate schools. Public school supporters are those who are not separate-school supporters.

In the procedures of a separate-school board, all the matters discussed concern all trustees. A public board, however, comprises two classes of trustees; one class elected by public school supporters (who direct their property taxes for the support of elementary and secondary schools); and one class elected by separate school supporters (who direct their property taxes for the support of secondary schools only). Hence, a meeting of a public board has a double agenda: those items dealing exclusively with the public schools, on which only the first-named class of trustees may vote; and items not dealing exclusively with the public schools, on which both classes of trustees may vote. Thus, in law, if not in practice, the Education Act, Section 209, subsection 1 calls for:

> two budget estimates, to be voted upon in two distinct motions. One of the estimates is for public-school purposes and the other is for secondary-school purposes. The board cannot have one whole budget, for if it were done in this way a separate-school rate-payers' representative would be required to vote on the expenditure and allocation of taxes collected exclusively from public-school supporters (Gilbert *et al.*, 1984).*

The organizational structure of a typical board of education includes a chief education officer. This senior civil servant is the director of education and secretary-treasurer of the board; below the director are usually several superintendents, depending upon the size of the board. The director and superintendents are supervisory officers.

We shall take as an example a board of education in a mid-sized rural-urban county in Ontario. The county town has a population of approximately 40,000, about half that of the county. A superintendent of business, who is not a certificated teacher, has authority over finances, plant, pur-

---

* Recent political developments may alter this present arrangement.

chasing and transport, through various assistant superintendents, controllers and managers. The academic division has five superintendents. One is in charge of curriculum, and four designated as superintendents of instruction. The superintendent of curriculum is in charge of the general curriculum, and the media centre, and the field station. Each superintendent of instruction has general charge of the schools in an area within the county. In addition, one or two are assigned special responsibilities (for example, community services). Principals normally report to the board through the appropriate superintendent. Usually all principals in an area meet regularly to discuss common concerns.

This arrangement has a hierarchy of authority, neatly arranged. The director of education is at the top, and the staff and pupils of each school are at the bottom of the pyramid. In handbooks, the organization chart lists their responsibilities, including those imposed by the various acts and regulations. At times, the duties even seem to contradict each other; for example, in the case of a pupil's suspension, The Education Act places the authority on the principal; in some jurisdictions, however, board policy names the appropriate (geographically speaking) superintendent as the final arbiter.

In a large jurisdiction, the same principles apply, but inevitably there are more superintendents. These come in two ranks: super-superintendents with jurisdiction over geographical areas, with more specialized supervisory officers beneath them; or superintendents of curriculum, personnel, professional services and the like, together with some area superintendents, to whom lesser superintendents report. Some boards have as many as twenty-two supervisors in the academic side of the board's operations.

The principals report to supervisory officers. Their responsibilities are prescribed both by the acts and regulations and by the board's policies. The Education Act, Section 236, charges principals with duties additional to those assigned to a teacher. These include directions regarding the mechanical side of the school: maintaining order, classifying pupils, keeping attendance and preparing timetables. As leaders they must also develop cooperation among the staff. The school should be the basic unit in the educational system; as many decisions as possible should be made by the professional staff, by the principal and the teachers. They must also accept responsibility for their decisions. Teachers must acknowledge that they are professionals. Such a concept needs changes in the fundamental structure and allocation of responsibilities, as well as in attitudes developed in faculties of education and within boards. A corollary would be a great diminution in the number of supervisory officers.

Separate Schools. Some, but not all, provinces have denominational schools. For example, Quebec and Newfoundland have denominational schools, whereas Ontario has a system of dissentient or public and separate schools. The Ontario separate schools may be Roman Catholic or Protestant, depending on the denomination of the public school. Simply put, there are two "official" religions: the first-comers or majority founded a public school; the later arrivals who dissented opened separate schools. Therefore, not all separate school boards are Roman Catholic; in fact, two boards are Protestant. Even some public schools are predominantly Roman Catholic. And some jurisdictions have only public schools because of an insufficient number of dissentients to support such a separate school board.

These school systems are complementary. Both share in the public purse in one way or another; all teachers are similarly qualified; all boards, teachers and pupils are subject to the same laws. There is one important distinction in organizational structure, however. Separate schools were originally for pupils in grades 1 to 8 inclusive. After the extension of the right of some public schools to teach grades 9 and 10, the same right was eventually (in the 1890's) extended to separate schools. In 1971, the secondary schools as a whole were also brought under the control of public boards. Thus, we have the anomalous situation of a public system from grades 1 to 13, but a separate school system from grades 1 to 10. Grades above grade 10 in a Roman Catholic school are not taught in the separate school system, but are part of a private school, unsupported in any way by public funding. In addition, the grade 9 and 10 pupils are still regarded, because of the historical development, as elementary school pupils and the boards receive grants accordingly. At present, the difference amounts to about $1000 per pupil per year. It should be noted, however, that the Education Amendment Act, 1981 (special education) provides equal funding of public- and separate-school special pupils, regardless of grade level.

In addition to the discussion of separate schools referred to earlier in the Report of the Royal Commission on Education in Ontario (1950), another source of information may be found in *A Hard Act To Follow* (Gilbert *et al.*, 1984).

6.2   Financing Education

Because of the political overtones, changes frequently occur in the principles and practices of school funding. We shall discuss first where the money comes from and who allocates it, then briefly examine spending within a school, so that teachers may have some knowledge about how money is made available for their needs.

There is a strong tradition for public support of education. It increases as the society becomes more democratically based. Writing about Ontario, Saunders (1970) remarks that

> Education in Ontario is a function of local government carried out by school boards on behalf of the provincial government. Education has been offered without cost to students since 1871 in elementary, and since 1921 in secondary schools. Separate school boards, public school boards and boards of education are elected locally now, although until 1968 the old district high school boards were appointive. Ontarians assume, rightly, that by making education a local responsibility the schools will reflect better the needs and interests of the community, and the tradition of local self-government in education is strong.

Indeed, local boards have more closely reflected local needs in the years since Saunders wrote those words. Increasing costs, declining enrolment and economic hard times have brought local and provincial financing under very close and continuous scrutiny.

In general, schools operate on funds provided by local taxes ("rates") and provincial grants. This has been true since the earliest days, although the bases upon which both were collected have changed frequently. For a number of years, fees were also charged directly. More recently, the provincial government has somehow adopted a "Robin Hood style"; some boards, notably in larger urban areas, receive a smaller percentage of their total expenses than do rural boards in areas with limited assessment. Various plans have tried to equalize the ability of boards to cope with fiscal matters. In 1964, for example, a wholesale revision of the structure was put into effect to satisfy the needs of boards. Among other changes, the province undertook

> to pay at least 35 percent of (recognized extraordinary expenditure) plus equalization grants based on assessment per classroom. In addition, a veritable jungle of stimulation and special grants for evening courses, library books, milk, municipal inspectors' salaries, special education programs, etc., was created, all of which complicated the grant system and tended to reward the wealthier areas willing to establish these programs. The provincial government in effect guaranteed minimum expenditure levels through these grants while leaving to school boards considerable discretionary authority over the ultimate allocation of resources to educational services (Saunders, 1970).

Generally speaking, boards of education have rights of taxation limited only by political reality. Between 1971-75, the province of Ontario imposed spending ceilings. The competition for tax money became intense and education had to compete with other sources, for example, health progams and welfare costs. The ceilings determine ordinary expenditure per pupil, with elementary and secondary pupils being rated differently. Expenditures also depend on location and certain programs. The ceilings were increased in succeeding years, but as Stewart (1972) notes: "the departmental ceilings do not cause a decrease in the amount of money spent per student, but rather the rate of increase is decreasing."

This approach had its problems. The ceilings rose, but not at pace with inflation. But the teachers demanded salary increases to keep up with inflation. And all expenditures for boards were increasing, although salaries constituted by far the largest portion.

Eventually, the ceilings were removed. Now, two other factors disturbed the relatively tranquil scene; first, the wage controls of 1975, and then, the steady reduction of provincial government funding. The latter caused some boards to raise local rates. Many were reluctant to do so for fiscal and political reasons. Then, beginning around 1977, declining enrolment and the closing of schools intruded upon the fiscal scene; many rate-payers who expected correspondingly lower local taxes were disappointed. Strikes by teachers at this time secured higher wage settlements, but at the cost of alienating public support. Consequently, boards were under pressure to keep tax rates down, as noted in the *Toronto Star*, July 25, 1977:

School taxes leap as enrolment drops: taxpayers ask why? ... Along with other rate payers from across Metro — 10,000 have signed a petition condemning the jump in the mill rate — [X] rushed to do battle with the educational establishment, armed with a host of angry questions, chief of which was "Why are educational costs continuing to rise when enrolment is declining?"

An uneasy truce prevails today as boards have more-or-less convinced rate-payers that things are not so simple. Debentures must still be paid off and teachers' salaries must increase because of additional qualifications, and few young (and therefore relatively inexpensive) teachers are hired. Energy bills are high, and schools still cost as much to heat even though they are only half-full. Nevertheless, fiscal responsibility is still a priority among trustees and would-be trustees. The campaign literature collected during the municipal elections of 1982 bears this out:

- [X] believes that a cost increase of 20 percent per pupil each year over the past five years should have resulted in a noticeable improvement in the quality of education (Candidate in Toronto).
- support for the government's wage restraint program (Metropolitan Separate School Board).
- exercise restraint in spending wherever possible... our education budget should reflect declining enrolment (Etobicoke).

Of course, financial restraint is only one pressing need acknowledged by the public. As lowered spending becomes a priority, it will engender tension among educational authorities as they battle for their share. The introduction of extended special education facilities and programs will heighten the competition. All this could increase pressure for more central funding or a revamped system of taxation to shift some burden away from local rate-payers by changing the property tax system. Given the historical roots of the latter system, however, it is unlikely to happen in the present political climate.

Finances Within the School. Many teachers are unaware of exactly how finances are handled in their school. If they want supplies, they follow the established routine, without really thinking about how they became available. For textbooks, or similar items, they usually turn to a department head, grade chairman, vice-principal or principal.

A better understanding of internal finances would promote a greater sense of responsibility, and hence professionalism, for the teacher. Financial affairs should be open to all professional staff. It is encouraging to note that boards and superintendents are increasingly allowing principals more fiscal autonomy with no loss of accountability. Principals, in turn, often bring senior teachers into consultation, or even turn over the allocation of money to a small committee.

Each school receives its funds from the board in the form of an annual budget. Usually the amount is determined by two factors: first, the amount allocated per pupil and then, the actual enrolment. It is the responsibility of the principals or their designates to allocate the money.

For example, a typical secondary school with about 1300 to 1400 pupils has a final budget of about $200,000. Most of this money is a basic allocation, with additional sums for certain activities (special education, night school, for example). The budget is allocated by areas, including subject departments, the administrative side of the school, textbooks, the library, the audio-visual services and so on. Across all these areas, there is usually a division into supplies (consumable items) and capital expenses (equipment). Machines used in common (micro-computers, photocopiers, word processors, for example) are often listed as a separate item. These add about 10 per cent to the budget. Some areas—science, technical education, art, physical education, music—are big spenders. Textbooks and the library expenses account for large portions of the budget, as do general supplies and office administration. Some departments (history, modern languages, classical languages, for example) require relatively small budgets; on the other hand, "newer" subjects, generally speaking, cost more.

Other items in the budget include expenses for telephones, postage, transport, (non-food) cafeteria supplies, and special occasions such as parents' night and commencement. There is usually an amount available for assistance to students in need and some principals keep back some money for contingencies.

Teachers should study the budget system within the school, whatever its size or nature, and the channels to use to request supplies and equipment. The dates by which requests are required are also important. In these days of careful budgeting, they must not only meet all deadlines but also propose good arguments in support of each request. They should take care to request only equipment that is absolutely necessary; many a classroom in the province has seldom-used equipment stored in the corner.

6.3   Advisory Committees

From time to time, attempts are made to draw the community into the making of decisions that affect the day-to-day operations of the school. This trend was particularly noticeable in the early 1970's when the concept of parental participation was at its strongest. Of course, some structures are in place to work with the school. (They will be discussed more fully in the following section.) These home and school or parent-teacher associations generally have never been decision-making bodies, not even advisory bodies. "Advisory committee" usually means a group, body, duly constituted by the minister under the Education Act, that represents various groups within and outside the school; it is empowered to advise the principal of the school about certain designated matters.

Some have suggested that more substantial powers be given to such committees; in practice, however, these ideas have not been given serious consideration except in isolated occasions. At the height of the agitation for more involvement by parents and rate-payers, the boards established committees to help choose principals for schools. One or two did actually meet but their efficacy was doubtful and the committees dissolved in confusion. It was difficult to reconcile the various constitu-

Your Education Investment

A	Instruction	69.6%
B	Educational and Pupil Welfare Services	3.5%
C	Administration and Computer Services	2.4%
D	Plant Operations	12.5%
E	Plant Maintenance	6.7%
F	Pupil Transportation, cafeteria and Other Services	1.9%
G	Capital Expenditure from Current Funds	3.4%

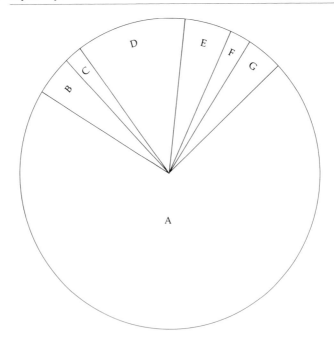

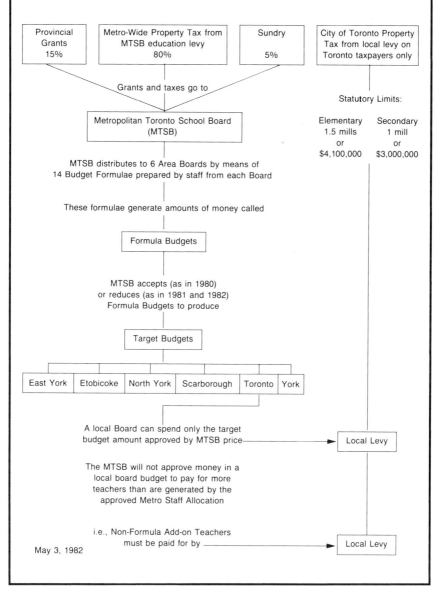

Where does the money come from?

Sources of Financing of Public Education in Toronto-1982

| Provincial Grants 15% | Metro-Wide Property Tax from MTSB education levy 80% | Sundry 5% | City of Toronto Property Tax from local levy on Toronto taxpayers only |

Grants and taxes go to

Metropolitan Toronto School Board (MTSB)

Statutory Limits:

	Elementary	Secondary
	1.5 mills	1 mill
	or	or
	$4,100,000	$3,000,000

MTSB distributes to 6 Area Boards by means of 14 Budget Formulae prepared by staff from each Board

These formulae generate amounts of money called

Formula Budgets

MTSB accepts (as in 1980) or reduces (as in 1981 and 1982) Formula Budgets to produce

Target Budgets

| East York | Etobicoke | North York | Scarborough | Toronto | York |

A local Board can spend only the target budget amount approved by MTSB price————▶ Local Levy

The MTSB will not approve money in a local board budget to pay for more teachers than are generated by the approved Metro Staff Allocation

i.e., Non-Formula Add-on Teachers must be paid for by ————▶ Local Levy

May 3, 1982

encies (parents, teachers, pupils) and their vested interests.* More fundamentally, the educational system has always been highly centralized. It was probably too difficult to overcome the cultural inertia inherent in such a state of affairs. Opposition members introduced private member's bills into the legislative assembly in the early 1970's. These sought to establish advisory committees for individual schools, but they languished on the order paper. The government did amend the (then) Schools' Administration Act to allow the establishment of a School Board Advisory Committee. This idea has been carried on in the Education Act (Secs. 177-181). In the execution, however, the committees have turned out to be toothless tigers.

The committees have different structures, according to the kind of board. All boards are composed of three members of the board appointed by the board; the chief education officer of the board or his nominee; six teachers hired by the board, appointed by the teachers in the employ of the board; four persons appointed by the board who are neither teachers nor members of a board, but who are resident within the jurisdiction of the board; and the persons appointed under subsections (2) and (3). Subsections (2) and (3) note special representation in the case of separate school boards, and of parent-teacher associations and home and school councils respectively. Pupils and ancillary staff are not represented.

Advisory committees have the power to make reports and recommendations "in respect of any educational matter pertaining to the schools under the jurisdiction of the board" (Sec. 181), with the exception of personnel and salary matters.

Other advisory committees established in the Education Act have quite specific functions. The Special Education Advisory Committee (Section 182) serves exceptional children. It consists of three board members, up to 12 members representing special-interest associations, together with provision for French- or English-speaking representatives, as the case may be. The Educational Act (Sec. 262-270) also establishes French-language advisory committees where conditions permit. Such committees consist of three board members and six French-speaking rate-payers elected by French-speaking rate-payers in the secondary school district concerned. Section 267 of the Act outlines fourteen items for the committee to concern itself with, ranging from textbooks and sites to adult education programs. Many would like to see such advisory powers strengthened in all advisory committees and passed on to individual school committees.

* Some boards have re-established this procedure.

6.31 A Model from England and Wales*

The Education Act, 1944 (England and Wales) gave local education authorities power to establish boards of governors (for secondary schools) and boards of managers (for elementary schools). Although these powers were not always exercised, in many cases boards were established. More recently the United Kingdom government established a committee to study the school boards; its report was made public in September 1977.

> Whatever the government, the local council and the education experts between them decide about schools in general, every school is a special place, the school around somebody's corner. No two schools have exactly the same needs or problems and that is why the first recommendation of my committee is that every school, big or small, should have its own governors to look after its interests.

This is the basic premise of the recommendations of the Taylor Committee. (See *Times Educational Supplement*, September 23, 1977.) The recommendations are summarized in the following eight paragraphs.

Curriculum. This involves establishment of the school's objectives; sharing in the formation of the structure of learning, care and rules needed to achieve these objectives; constantly reviewing the school's success in achieving its objectives and producing regularly more formal appraisals of its performance; and having access, in its task, to the professional guidance of advisors (consultants) and inspectors.

Behaviour in Schools. The governors should ensure that, in all its activities, the school encourages good behaviour. They make the rules that deal with departures from such standards. They also ensure that school policies on discipline are understood, and encourage the pupils, parents and the community to support these policies.

Finance. Governing bodies should be involved as fully as possibly in preparing estimates and budgeting for their schools. Because they know exactly how the money is allocated and can set out their own priorities before decisions are made, the governors should, as much as possible, prepare the budget.

Appointments and Dismissals. Governors should share, on equal terms with the local education authority, the responsibility for selecting head teachers, and should have formal responsibility as a body even if they in

---

* Much of the material in the remaining part of this section is taken verbatim from Gilbert, V. K. *Comment on Education.*

practice delegate it for the choice of other staff, including non-teaching staff.

Admissions, Suspensions, and Expulsions. No child should be debarred from school (other than on medical grounds) except in accordance with procedures established by the local education authority, and no child expelled except by decision of the local education authority.

Schools Premises and Holidays. Parents must have adequate access to the school for their activities, within a general policy of making school facilities as widely available to the community as possible. In the past governors could grant occasional holidays. They should continue this practice, as long as these were occasions of special importance to the school, and the variations within an area did not cause undue inconvenience for parents, local industry, or the services common to several schools.

Procedures. The Commission recommended governors should elect their own chairman to the board provided that no employee of the school concerned could serve as chairman. The governors' term of office should be about four years. It was not possible to be precise because of varying election intervals, the fact that parents' eligibility depended on having children at the school, and that some areas wished to provide for a two-year break for teacher representatives to ensure that they represented a changing staff.

They should meet at least twice a term. The proceedings should not be confidential unless in any particular case the governors themselves so decided.

There should be no attendance allowances for governors (some councillors are paid such allowances at present). Local education authorities should arrange compensation for loss of earnings (provided meetings were held at times convenient to a majority of members), and should pay travel expenses for all classes of governors. No governor should be prevented from serving because of the cost of attending regular meetings. The local education authority should decide upon the clerking arrangements for governing bodies in their areas. Some provide clerks from their offices, some use school secretaries, and others allow governors to appoint their own clerk from among their number.

The New Governors. One quarter of each governing body should represent the local education authority. The second quarter should represent the staff, including the head teacher and elected representatives of the teaching staff, and in larger schools, of the ancillary staff. The third quarter should be elected by all the parents of children attending the school. In some cases, pupils are eligible to serve as full governors; such pupils are elected by their fellows. The final quarter, co-opted by the other three groups, should represent the local community.

Although these are recommendations of a commission, the general principles already exist in practice; the report sought to modify in some respects and extend powers in others. The main thrust has been towards making proceedings more open to the public.

The powers of the boards of governors appear quite broad; in practice, most of them are exercised by the head teacher. Head teachers use the boards to gather some measure of public opinion or support. This system does not really need a hierarchy of superintendents; their responsibilities devolve upon the boards and the head teacher. Head teachers are permitted to exercise duties defined in the Education Act, and do not need supervision except in a very general way. On specific, local affairs, the board acts in this capacity.

Although Canadian schools have, for the most part, adopted the industrial model of organization, it could be replaced by a more professional structure, like the one recommended above.

6.32 A New Model for School Committees

Powers
Most powers and responsibilities could be adopted in their entirety from the Taylor recommendations.

Composition
40 per cent—members of divisional board of education, or persons appointed by them
25 per cent—staff, including principal, ex-officio and where practicable, non-teaching staff
25 per cent—parents of pupils, elected by all parents
10 per cent—pupils, where of suitable age, otherwise 30 per cent staff, 30 per cent parents

In a committee of 12, this arrangement would provide
5 representing the board of education
3 staff (principal, 1 teacher and 1 non-teacher)
3 parents
1 pupil (of age 18)

In a committee of 20, the composition would be:
8 appointed by the board of education
5 staff
5 parents
2 pupils

These suggestions need to be accompanied by changes in attitude among the boards of education. They would be concerned more with policy decisions on a larger scale, yet keep control of individual committees through fiscal policies. Superintendents could be reduced, but consultants would be necessary for working with principals and committees.

Such a system of school committees would return the authority over the school to the local community, in a democratic way, without the danger of lobbies gaining control. It would also avoid those situations where the superintendents are merely super-principals. Even though they have begun to decentralize authority, in practice they may have become even more centralized. There is also the possibility sometimes, even, a single trustee can gain control over schools by manipulating a superintendent—this is much easier to do with one person than with a group of principals.

There are inherent differences that might hinder the adoption *in toto* of the governors'/managers' model. The most serious is the size of the elected local authority. Councils which control education through a large education committee can be quite large. Fifty or sixty members is not uncommon. This makes it relatively easy to appoint one or two councillors to a multitude of school boards.

But there is one Ontario model with fiscal autonomy and the powers described above that has few elected members—the public library boards in Ontario each have only one elected trustee (the mayor or representative). Up to eight other members are appointed by the boards of education and the municipal council concerned. The only legal accountability is in the process of pursuing a grant for the annual budget from the municipal council. Only at this stage are questions asked.

The new committees would have less authority, and they would be subject to policies laid down by the boards of education. This kind of decentralization, coupled with the rising authority of the teachers' federations, could inspire more professionalism in teaching. Another benefit is that it involves many more people, from all walks of life, in the governance of schools.

6.33 Associations Linking Parents and Schools

Independent (private) schools rely almost exclusively on parents for funding, whether through fees or supplementary methods. But these associations rarely influence education decisions. To use the medical analogy, would hospital volunteers debate professional matters with the chief medical officer or the hospital's board of directors?

Undoubtedly, parent-school associations were influenced by the volunteer movements of the nineteenth century when citizens helped with prisons, hospitals and other public institutions. From humble beginnings, usually fund raising for library books, gymnasium equipment, or uniforms, the associations now play an influential part in education. Some areas have very strong parent-school associations.

The Canadian Home and School and Parent-Teacher Federation (CHSPTF) has constituent organizations in all provinces and territories. The first association was founded in Baddeck, N.S., in 1895, under the leadership of Mrs. Alexander Graham Bell. The general aims of the CHSPTF are that each member-organization:

Is concerned with all problems that relate to the welfare of the child in the home, school and community.

Strives to interest all people in all children, and to link in common purpose the home, the school and other educative forces in the life of the child, to work for the highest good.

Learns at first hand all school conditions which will ensure the growth and safety of the child.

Encourages all influences and conditions which will ensure the growth and safety of the child.

Works actively to supply the school and community needs by creating public sentiment which will favor and provide good teachers, good school equipment and adequate recreation for leisure time.

Gives service to the home by training for parenthood and homemaking and to the school by adding parent power to the school power.

Is a co-operative effort to produce Canadian citizens who shall be capable of perpetuating the best of our national life.

Promotes the study of issues related to the education and welfare of children and youth and after discussion presents considered proposals to appropriate authorities and levels of government.

On a national scale, the federation has worked in various activities to help children (smoking habits, International Year of the Child, as examples). Many of the federation's resolutions have been enacted by governments responsible; others continue to receive attention. A few such resolutions include:

Exemption from taxable income of tuition fees.

Mandatory instructions and examinations for school bus drivers.

Fireproofing of children's clothing.

Enforcement of the National Building Code as it relates to the handicapped.

Encouragement of the departments of education and school boards to buy textbooks written and published in Canada.

Safety standards for bicycles.

Membership in a local organization (in Ontario, a home and school association in public schools, a parent-teacher association in separate schools) provides many benefits to parents, teachers and pupils.

Parents Gain
- A chance to meet their children's teachers, to exchange valuable information.
- An understanding of essential study/work habits and needs.
- A better understanding of the child's stages and related growth and emotional problems.
- A chance to meet the parents of their children's classmates.
- A voice in shaping educational changes.
- An opportunity to know the educational channels open to children.
- An awareness of how they can help the teacher.
- A broad understanding of the education system and an appreciation of the need for parental involvement.

Teachers Gain
- Parental interest, understanding and support.
- Co-operation in establishing a common discipline.
- Enlistment of parental concern for the mental health and emotional growth of the child.
- An opportunity to interpret "education" to the parents.
- An opportunity to interpret new methods and curricular changes.
- Better understanding of each child through acquaintance with parents.

Students Gain
- Co-operation of parents and teachers in their best interest.
- Parental interest and involvement in home and school, parent-teacher work.
- Parental participation in their schools.

— A sense of security that their parents are interested in their development.
— Confidence in a uniform discipline and set of values.
— Guidance and encouragement from the combined wisdom of parents and teachers.

With respect to public relations, a home-and-school and parent-teacher group can provide a platform from which to launch ideas and a sounding board for the community's views. Frequently, a principal can enlist the help of members of an association for some political action, especially when the board of education or the municipal council is involved. Often, effective lobbying of councillors gets results.

In some schools, weak home-and-school and parent-teacher associations are frequently supplanted by parental groups formed for specific purposes or by increased school/parent consultations and interviews. For example, in Roman Catholic separate schools and private high schools groups of parents help the priests and teachers to guide the students' religious development: by preparing them for First Communion and Confirmation, and setting up special liturgies, and series of lectures or seminars on spiritual topics or current educational issues. It is unclear how much such groups and interests supplant the formal groups.

6.4   The Formal Structure: The Principal's Place
in the School Hierarchy
The position of the principal in the hierarchy of education has changed dramatically since the 1960's. Before then, the principals had almost absolute authority. Then authority was seldom, if ever, challenged.

Today, the position has changed and its authority has greatly eroded. The geographical areas under the school boards have become much bigger. Few principals deal directly with the board anymore. There are often two or three levels of supervisory offices between the principal and the board. At one time, the ministry scarcely recognized the existence of supervisory officers; now it grants them authority over the principal. The teachers' federations show less and less respect for the position of the principal. The salary gap between the classroom teacher and the principal has narrowed through lack of protection of the principal's position in negotiations and contracts have clauses which greatly reduce the rights of the principals even to deploy staff in the school according to their own wishes. The public also seems to have less respect for the principal's position as a figure in authority.

How does the principal deal with various agencies in education—the ministry, school board, supervisory officers, teachers' federations, principals' or headmasters' organizations, the public, the school staff, and students?

The Ministry. Through the government and legislature, the education ministry initiates the acts and regulations under which a principal operates a school. There have been subtle changes over the years but, except for the introduction of the supervisory officer's authority over the principal, there is little in the acts and regulations about which many principals would complain. The principal does have much authority. The ministry insists on reports, many of which are long and tedious to complete, but little could change without altering the way schools are financed. Many principals want to be consulted more before changes are made in compulsory programs. For their part, however, the ministry could show they do in fact consult with some principals and it is impossible to consult with them all. Public education has always carried with it political overtones.

School Boards. Until recently, school boards dealt with the finances and left the running of the school to the professionals. The board received reports about programs but seldom made major changes. Over the past twenty years, however, there have been more and more questions and demands. To their discredit, the professionals are more and more defensive and even deceitful about school operations. In turn, the boards become even more suspicious and questioning. The professionals pull back into defensive posture and even look as if they were covering up. And so it goes on. The advent of full-time trustees has accelerated the process.

Meanwhile, the principals, who seldom deal directly with the board anymore, are caught in the middle. They cannot easily go over the heads of the supervisory officers to answer questions from the board. They are not treated as the middle management that they are, possibly because principals are members of the federation that seems at war with the boards from time to time. So, the board cannot easily consult the principals, and the principals cannot easily reach the board.

Supervisory Officers. The superintendents are unfortunately not as close to the principals as they should be. It is not just a problem of getting along with the boss. (The superintendent does indeed write the evaluation reports about the principal.) It seems to be deeper than that—really a question of local autonomy. The principals want the authority to run the schools as they see fit. After all, who can best understand the true needs of the school? The superintendents seem to want all schools to be alike, or at least to operate uniformly, under a set of operating procedures written by the superintendent. In contrast to the acts and regulations of the ministry, the policies and operating procedures written by the superintendent and authorized by the Board are much more prescriptive. The principals see little room to operate. Rightly or wrongly, they feel a lack of faith and trust from those they work for.

A major problem is in the area of school management. Superintendents advise the board negotiating team. They seldom consult with the principals because the principals are "federation." Thus, clauses are written into contracts that make the running of the school very difficult, but there is almost no consultation with the branch manager—the principal.

The Teachers' Federations. As a federation member, the principals often pay the highest individual fees to the organization (where fees are based on salary level). Many believe that they should be highly respected members of the organization because they have always been among the strongest supporters. However, as the federations have become more union-like, they have become suspicious of all levels of management, including the principals. This is unfair to these very loyal members, and is also causing problems in the schools between the staff and the principal.

From the position of the principal, the situation is quite contentious. Treated like members of a federation by the superintendents and the board, and treated like management by the federation, the principal is in the middle again. When principals offer advice, they are regarded as meddlers by both parties. Therefore, they speak only when spoken to. What a waste of talent. No one is in a better position to remedy the problems between the boards and the federations—the middle position could be one of great strength.

Principals' or Headmasters' Organizations. Here lies a solution to the many problems in education, if only these organizations could show stronger leadership.

The Public. The public has always looked to principals for leadership and guidance. Unfortunately, it is hard for the principals to reach the public in a way that has any real meaning. Nevertheless, the principals must keep the parents, and the public in general, informed about school matters.

Staff. Almost all principals can work well with the staff in their own schools. Cases of difficulties between staff and principal are rare. As long as the principals communicate well with the staff and invite them to be involved with the development of school programs and policies, then there will be reasonable rapport. No principal can be all things to all staff. Sometimes they must say "No" and there is no good way of doing that. But the principals must take the time to explain positions.

Students. Here it is very much like the situation with the staff. The principal represents discipline, veto power, restrictions and some students will never be able to accept the need. As long as the principals are fair and work in the best interests of the students, and take time to explain what is going on, then the atmosphere will generally be favourable.

If the principals do not take a strong enough role with the outside agencies — the ministry, the board, the superintendent, the federations — the students may feel let down. The principals must be strong leaders. No amount of explaining will erase the problem of a seemingly weak leader. The principals must speak strongly on behalf of the students, and for the benefit of education in general.

6.5   Students' Councils

The role of students' government is not well defined; the responsibilities vary widely. Loosely speaking, the students' council is an extra-curricular side of a school. This view does not take into account the political connotations when students are drawn into running or assisting activities within the school. Students' councils are rare in elementary schools, although pupils are frequently encouraged to help in specific programs (road crossing duties, Junior Red Cross, for example); accordingly, this discussion will be limited to the formal students' council organization in secondary schools.

There is little, if any, legal provision for the establishment of students' governing bodies. Boards of education may have general policies towards them, but nowhere is it immediately apparent in the acts or regulations that there is a right to organize in this fashion. Neither, for that matter, is there any prohibition. Students' governments exist by custom, hallowed by time. Few secondary schools, at least in the public sector, are without some form of elected body. The general form of approval comes under the sanctioning by the board of education of extra-curricular activities in general.

With the years, and especially in recent times, the functions of students' councils have changed. Before, they were vehicles through which pupils learned of the various activities and many of them were organized.

Now in many schools, councils take part in discussion about policies within the school. It is not legally permissible for principals to delegate responsibility for policy-making to the pupils. Still, prudent principals encourage, at the very least, some contributions from this important group.

The prime functions of students' councils are still in extra-curricular activities, with a heavy emphasis on athletic and social events. There are the additional implied goals of practising democracy and learning good citizenship. A lofty goal, the latter, and achievement depends heavily upon the willingness of the principal and staff to give real responsibilities to the council. The staff sponsors are crucial here: they must take the job seriously yet not seem to be interfering in the routine affairs of the council. It is not easy to do. As Frederick (1965) describes it:

> Student council faculty advisors should be sympathetic with the ideas of student government, loyal to students and the administration, able to win confidence and respect, possess a sense of relative values, courage to allow some mistakes to be made by students, a genuine spirit of cooperation, resistance to discouragement, a genius for listening, courage to try the new and different and a desire to learn.

The appointment of a staff sponsor is one important way the principal establishes contact with the pupils. Many principals overlook this. Often, to be elected, the members must meet certain academic qualifications. Often, too, the principal retains a power of veto. Such restrictions, if used too freely, could turn a students' council into a rubber stamp for the principal.

The organization of most students' councils has changed little over the past decades, despite differences in political climates and relationships in schools. The traditional structure included a written constitution, and clearly defined responsibilities and relationships with the adminstrative structure of the school. Usually, several standing committees are defined; often qualifications are listed for the various executive positions to which students may be elected. The traditional form of council has been based on the home-room as the constituency, with an executive elected at large, as in a local government election (mayor and board of control, for example). This form of government has remained popular; it satisfies the majority of pupils and teaches those who take part something of the democratic system and parliamentary practices. (A knowledge of such procedures is of inestimable value in any form of organized group.) Even after the 1960's, with the attendant activism, some new forms of government emerged. Most were a re-definition of the parts played by the council in the daily affairs of the school.

In a typical 1200-pupil secondary school, a students' council (almost invariably named the Students' Administrative Council or SAC) consists of the following:

- The executive, comprising a
  president
  vice-president(s)
  secretary
  treasurer
  Boys' Athletic Association president
  Girls' Athletic Association president
  and other special positions.

  The total runs from about six to as many as fifteen.

- Representatives, usually one from each home form. The number can run from about twenty-five to forty, or more.

The SAC can be a body of as few as 30, or as large as 65 to 70, depending on the size of the school. The larger council resembles a small parliament; here, without well-defined party policies, the work of the council usually devolves upon the executive, for it is difficult for seventy independents to agree to an agenda.

Another model for a students' council is based upon the house structure within the school. In this case, the school is already divided for "pastoral" purposes into, say, six houses, each with its own council to deal with house affairs. These councils are formed in a fashion similar to that described above, except that the executive is smaller. The school council in this case comprises an executive of six or eight elected by the whole school, and representatives of each house, one a senior, one a junior student (elected by the house). In this case there is an SAC of about eighteen to twenty members. This is a much more manageable size.

To practise more responsibility, a students' council can be given control of the activity fee money, as well as the task of collecting it. In this regard, the staff sponsor with the SAC treasurer is important. Clubs that want money from the SAC must formally request it and the council decides in the best interests of the school.

The SAC can also, to some extent, decide which clubs may operate in the school. A useful device incorporates a double veto; that is, a club must have the approval of both the principal and the SAC. This system gives the SAC a status in the eyes of the students.

The councils are excellent forums for introducing young people to the realities of government. They provide links between the principal and the staff, and the pupils. They enable the principal, through the SAC leaders and the staff sponsor, to be informed. Many young people have sound ideas about the school; it is a pity to waste them because there was no legitimate avenue for them to reach the right place.

Students' councils foster cooperation and a greater sense of participation on the part of students in the life of the school. The wise principal will use this in the best interests of everyone in the school—principal, staff, students and parents.

6.6   Relationships with Organizations External to the School

Often outside organizations approach the school for assistance either as a charity or else as a business venture. Occasionally, it is difficult to draw the line between the two, when the outside organization offers some rewards, tangible and intangible, to the students who become agents for them.

In the relatively innocent days before the 1960's, it was easy to decide, for these activities had gone on for many years. United Appeal and its predecessors, the Red Cross, department store clubs, religious groups—all had their places in schools. The political activism of the 1960's, however, changed relationships. Schools faced groups that had no allegiance to the schools, with rules and objectives drawn up outside the school, outside the control of the students' council, the principal, or the board.

Many boards passed regulations forbidding "school" clubs that belonged to organizations subject to external policy-making boards, and whose membership was determined by the parent group. While the policy was directed mainly at political groups, it also affected the department store clubs and other similar activities. Others, such as religious groups, survived because it was considered they were not affiliated in a formal way and that membership was determined within the school.

It would seem advisable in a school supported by public money that no clubs be formed that are affiliated directly with other bodies. However, activities connected with charities can remain autonomous and simply be vehicles for collection of funds. It is up to the SAC to permit them and to decide how the funds raised will be distributed.

Principals and students' councils should avoid organizations that run events or vacation trips for profit. They can use the school building, but only after a permit from the board, and certainly not in school time.

The board does have the right to decide who may advertise in a school. Section 26 of Regulation 262 states that:

No advertisement or announcement shall be placed in a school or on school property or distributed or announced to the pupils on school property without the consent of the board that operates the school except announcements of school activities.

In many cases, it delegates to the principal the right to decide on advertising for certain organizations (for example, home and school, parent-teacher associations, United Appeal, scouts, guides, local churches and synagogues).

6.7   Alternative Structures

6.71   Private Schools
The term "school" is defined in the Education Act to be:

(i) the body of public school pupils or separate school pupils or secondary school pupils that is organized as a unit for educational purposes under the jurisdiction of the appropriate board, or

(ii) the body of pupils enrolled in any of the elementary or secondary school courses of study in an educational institution operated by the Government of Ontario (Sec. I, 1, 49).

A "private school" means

an institution at which instruction is provided at any time between the hours of 9 a.m. and 4 p.m. on any school day for five or more pupils who are of or over compulsory school age in any of the subjects of the elementary or secondary school courses of study and that is not a school as defined in this section (Sec. I, 1, 40).

The difference is that "schools" are funded by public money and "private schools" are not. This distinction by no means explains the real differences between them. Private schools have their roots deep in the history of education before the "schools" as defined in the Act. The state is a relative newcomer to educational governance. Indeed, the distinction between "private" and "public" with respect to schools in British usage, from which many of the traditions of private schools in Ontario sprang, is in the form of ownership; that is, a private school is privately owned, a public school has some other form of ownership (for example, a foundation or a church). The term "independent school" is used as a collective term for these two groups of schools. This book uses the term "private school" in the Ontarian sense; but many who are associated with them use the term "independent school".

Private schools (exluding vocational schools) in Ontario number about 600. Some are quite small; others have many hundreds of pupils. One large class of private school comprises the upper grades of the Roman Catholic system; that is, the grades beyond 10, where public financial support as separate schools ceases. (This would change if the schools accept the government's offer of funding for grades 11-13.) Other religious groups operate private schools directly, still others are oriented towards certain denominational backgrounds but are legally independent of the churches.

All private schools charge fees, ranging from a few hundred dollars to five or six thousand a year. Why would parents, who already pay school taxes, pay to have their children educated in a private school? The most obvious reason is that of religious orientation. Many parents who believe that education should be based upon a religious foundation do not see such a condition in the public or secondary schools. Some are founded on unique educational approaches, for example, the Montessori schools. Some are based upon the appeal of the individual expertise of those who teach there. Others cater to those who wish to upgrade themselves in a short time, or for those who are considered "bright." One such school offers itself to those "who want to experience something refreshingly different in a high school and who want to develop their individual talents more completely than they have to date in regular schools."

Parents choose religiously-based schools for the value systems that come with the school. Parents who enrol their children in a church school expect them to study religion and attend religious services from time to time. Teachers at such schools must respect at least the values that are being inculcated, if not indeed take part in the process.

As the name "independent school" implies, the principal or governing body may hire persons who subscribe to their own views. This process may sound discriminatory, but it is not unlawful.

Some private schools have been criticized for being breeding grounds of snobbery. Their critics point to the high costs, which exclude most, and their enrolment, usually running in families, which implies an "old-boys' network" making it easier for those on the inside to achieve positions of responsibility in the outside world. No doubt knowing people helps. Nevertheless, parents will pay for special kinds of education, regardless of the overtones. At the present time, private education is flourishing as more and more parents send their children in the belief that the traditional values are instilled there.

One of the strongest attractions of the private school, over and above religious values, is that of a sense of belonging, of camaraderie. This is encouraged in every way and is perpetuated through Old Boys' and/or alumnae associations. This is one source of funding, and so becomes a major part of the school's continuing existence.

The organizational structures of private schools vary greatly. The older "traditional" schools are run much like the public ones. There is usually a principal or headmaster/mistress, sometimes a vice-principal and some-times, not always, department heads or the equivalent. Many such schools are based upon the house structure, particularly the boarding schools. The pastoral side of the school is usually highly developed; it is one way to transmit the values to the pupils. In the larger schools, a bursar man-ages the business affairs. This person is responsible to the principal, but works with teachers or department heads directly. The public school system could learn from the private schools in this regard. In his pro-posed reorganization of school administration, J. Lloyd Trump suggested that a business manager could relieve the principal of many non-teaching administrative tasks.

The old-line "traditional" private schools emphasize athletic and other activities in their curriculum; the way to a well-rounded person is through healthy activities that stimulate the body and the intellect. Some much smaller private schools have few, if any activities outside the class-room. Teachers and parents should investigate carefully that a particular school suits their needs before they accept a position or enrol their chil-dren. They should investigate the finances of less well-known schools. The ministry of education inspection covers only the curriculum, not the fiscal state. Some schools are owned by individuals or are subsidiaries of other companies; in these cases, business failure would leave employees without jobs and back-pay.

6.72   Alternative Schools

In one sense, the schools described in this chapter are an alterna-tive to those in the public sector. By-and-large, however, most private schools are not called "alternative" in the current use of the word. In-deed, because many alternative schools are funded with public money, the simple fact of private ownership is clearly not enough to establish the difference. It is in the structure, teaching methods, values and attitudes that there is a difference between a "traditional" and an alternative school.

No doubt there have always been those who were discontented about the methods or values in the public schools. Until the past twenty years, however, their only relief has been to seek—or establish—a private school that catered to their needs, whether they be parents or teachers. The most widely known school and one that has had considerable influence in many countries is, or was, Summerhill, a small boarding school in Essex (England). It was founded and operated by Alexander Sutherland Neill so that he could put into practice his views of freedom within a school context. Lessons were not compulsory; rules were made by the entire community (pupils and teachers) and enforced at weekly meetings. Transgressors were tried and punished by their peers. Neill believed it was living, not learning, that was of prime importance; the job of education is to develop the emotions. In a way, he institutionalized the non-school, in the style of Margaret Mead, who once noted "My grandmother wanted me to have an education, so she kept me out of school." Summerhill did have classes—teachers taught, but attendance was not compulsory. Children learnt only as they were motivated, whatever the reason; they themselves were free to decide when the time was ripe.

Obviously, Neill and Summerhill achieved some notoriety, much of it based on Neill's unusual academic approach. But he also was criticized for the moral standards at the school. He took a fairly liberal view, and on occasion, had to defend himself vigorously. There is extensive literature on the school. It was a lighthouse to the alternative school movement but it collapsed about three years after Neill's death in 1973. Such schools, founded on charismatic leadership, frequently fail to sustain themselves when the living force has gone. Nevertheless, similar schools sprang up all over the developed world—one near Orangeville, Ontario, (Everdale Place) had a brief but influential life around 1970. Trying to operate privately, it too went under.

In the 1960's, many other influences arose, based upon Neill's view that learning comes most easily when it is founded on curiosity or necessity. Any attempt of the educational system must not institutionalize on a massive scale this desire to learn. Compulsion leads only to boredom, apathy and in some cases, open rebellion. This attitude reflected the times—a period of general rebellion against authority, particularly in the United States during the Vietnam war when alternative schools were founded. There was also a great interest in education with an emphasis on the individual and a concern over perceived antiquated practices and attitudes. Many authors contributed to this philosophical approach. One of the more notable was Ivan Illich, a Roman Catholic priest, born in Austria but who became a U.S. citizen. He wrote and travelled out of an institution in Mexico, the Centre for Intercultural Documentation. He developed views along the lines of Margaret Mead and A. S. Neill. His most influential book was entitled *Deschooling Society.* His schema was built upon the non-use of schools as such. People of all ages would learn by moving about from one learning centre to another in the community — somewhat like using a library on a grand scale, where the resources of the whole community would be available through the use of counsellors. They would refer their clients to whatever source best suited their individual needs. The ordinary equipment in schools would be augmented by resources in the community — business, public institutions, services which would help people learn. Illich believed that most people learned what was most important to them outside the school system.

Given these streams of influence — Neill and Illich are only two of many writers — a new concept of education emerged; that is, that there must be some kind of option available not only privately but also through the public school sector. Many such schools were established to take care of unique local needs. Now, there is a recognizable group of characteristics that may be used to identify alternative schools. Smith (1973) provides the following list:

- They provide options within the public school system for pupils, parents and teachers.
- They are more responsive to the specific needs within the community than the conventional schools.
- Their goals seem more comprehensible than their public counterparts.
- They seek to develop individual talent and uniqueness.
- They encourage plurality and diversity.
- They seek to prepare their pupils for various roles in society.
- They are more flexible and therefore more responsive to change.
- They try a more humane approach.

Such schools allow different methods in education, including not only the curriculum but also contributions from the community in designing the curriculum, and the values and rules in the school. It is obviously necessary that the teachers understand the school and its environment.

Individual schools come and go in their own ways; some survive for years, others have a comparatively short life. The following are examples of form and process and not necessarily as schools still in existence. The information is taken largely from brochures published either by the board concerned or else by the school itself.

The most well-known and probably longest-living alternative school in metropolitan Toronto is SEED (Shared Experience, Exploration and Discovery). It "presents an informal approach to learning which allows students to pursue their own interests." The school began as an experimental summer program in 1968 (Summer of Exploration, Enquiry and Discovery), but by 1970 it had expanded (due to influences discussed earlier) into a full-time winter program. The school is based upon openness. One can see Neill's influence in the twice-weekly general meetings, with each person having an equal voice. There are few rules; those that do exist are set out by the community.

SEED is caught in a familiar problem; it is impossible to operate in the province without providing some form of credential. So, to award the Secondary School Honour Graduation Diploma, it has to have a "fairly traditional array of subjects" and a core group of certificated teachers. Other teaching is done using "catalysts" and "catalyst courses"; some of these courses are organized by the students who seek an expert to help, that is, to act as a catalyst. Other courses are offered by those with expertise who want to teach.

The Toronto board of education supports several alternative schools that cater to different interest groups. Some are designed for adults who have dropped out and wish to return (Contact School, The Students' School), others are for younger people, for example, Laneway Community School which began as a private school serving a housing area in the city. The program is individualized and remedial in nature, to teach people basic skills and subjects.

SOLE (School of Life Experience) is another alternative school that allows students to study academic subjects, usually at the advanced level, while learning how to operate a small business. Some business courses are at a general level and involve actual experience. The main learning style uses individualized instruction.

Other boards of education operate alternative schools. Peel County Board of Education runs IndEC (Independent Education Centre). In this secondary school the students are each responsible for their own learning. The curriculum is adapted to each student's needs and interests. The school uses community resources and encourages parents and other people to take part in the school's programs.

A discussion of alternative schools would be incomplete without a look at other sources. For example, the Parkway Program in Philadelphia was a somewhat different alternative. It drew its students from those who were "high risk" or disenchanted and could not adjust to regular school programs. These included gifted learners, academic failures, and disruptive pupils. The program was designed to take place mostly outside the school (it was known as the school without walls); it had a strong guidance and counselling focus along the lines of Illich's proposals and used community agencies and parents as much as possible. The program was aimed at preparing students, where possible, to re-enter a regular school program. There was a strong element of evaluation to deal with unmotivated young people who had dropped out of school.

Most private alternative schools have financial difficulties and must either close or else discover inventive ways of using their space and resources. It is difficult to operate a school for long on borrowed facilities and the goodwill of teachers. And schools in many different countries have had to cease operation.

The question remains whether alternative schools operated by publicly funded bodies and subject to controls imposed by them are really alternative. At the present, the alternative schools appear to be holding on to enough independence to maintain their credibility. They certainly provide an opportunity for those who need special attention; in their own way, they represent yet another facet of special education. They seem to have outlasted the radical beginnings.

7   Public Relations

7 Public Relations

7.1 The School and Communication with the Community

With the increasing complexity of society, the large school boards, and the growing criticism of education in general, it becomes more and more important for school administrators, principals and teachers to promote good public relations. They must assure the community that they are receiving good value for their money. Obviously, the best way to promote good public relations is to provide a sound education.

In consultation with staff the principal must choose what approach to take. In the "closed" approach, the school decides what is to be done and communicates those decisions to those concerned. In the "open" approach, those concerned take part in and contribute to the decisions. In between these two methods is a two-way communication between school and community; it is based upon a differentiation of decision-making between those items exclusively within the purview of the principals and those which they may conveniently delegate to others (Litwak and Meyer, 1965). Many principals opt for the latter, especially in Ontario.

To establish this "two-way" approach, it is necessary to set up channels of communication. Parker (1978) suggests eight ways to build this relationship between school and community:
- Find out what the community knows and thinks about its schools. Use surveys, interviews, and neighbourhood meetings to draw out suggestions and criticisms.
- Establish public relations priorities. Rank problems in order of gravity, and resolve them in that order.
- Develop a plan. Let the public know what problems are being dealt with. If the community knows it can play a part in the solutions, it will be less inclined to create problems.

- Appoint a public relations officer.
- Determine who in the community should receive appropriate information. Be sure to include senior citizens and childless couples. They also pay school taxes.
- "Show and tell" the story of your school. Let all residents and businesses know how they can help in the school.
- Listen to the views of the community. Listen to what the community thinks you are doing wrong as well as right.
- Handle the media with good sense. Make sure the press is the first, not the last, to know about your public relations.

Criscuolo (1977) suggests the following are characteristics of good public relations:

- The teachers have sympathetic attitudes towards those problems of the home that profoundly affect the education of a child.
- They are willing to listen to parents' ideas about teaching the child.
- They give the impression of accomplishing something worthwhile.
- They show enthusiasm for their work.
- They extend interest beyond the working day; for example, attend parent-teacher meetings and board meetings occasionally.
- They help children after school.

There are other means of communication besides using the teachers and the principals.

- People who work through the school—the psychologist, district public health nurse and social welfare agencies—can inform the public.
- It is also important to involve the "opinion leaders" in the community. These include the formal leaders, like the trustees, as well as businesspeople, and members of service clubs.
- School can reach out into the community either by being a community school or by using a settlement house approach.
- Voluntary associations (home and school or parent-teacher) are good vehicles but it is difficult to get all members to attend.
- Sending letters home is a good way of communicating because the school can control the message. However, many letters are lost or forgotten or ignored.
- Many schools do not take full advantage of the various media. What is the most appropriate medium depends on the message, the coverage desired, the cost, and who is to present the message. It is probably better to make selected attempts rather than attempt blanket coverage, for example:
  - a small weekly column in the local newspaper

- a major presentation for commencement
- presentation on community cable TV channels
- more imaginative uses of television—school activities, open houses
- local radio stations
- well-made posters and notices in supermarkets or other places where people congregate
- local newspaper columns for coming events
- The way discipline is applied can establish good relations. A just and consistent approach can go a long way.
- It is useful to know the community—what activities the residents find useful. Well-presented open houses, music nights, and athletic events are a great help. If music is "big," then put on a musical with a cast of hundreds.
- The reception parents and other visitors receive from staff, including secretaries in the office, makes a lasting impression. Courtesy costs nothing and reaps its own reward. Even the parking lot should be well maintained with clear directions and the school should have clear signs. Signs instructing that "Visitors Must Report to the Office", without indicating where the office is, are irritating and useless.
- Report cards are important for communication. They are frequently the only communication that is thoroughly examined by parents. Make it a good, informative instrument.

It is clear that every school activity can improve a school's image. Principals, teachers, ancillary personnel, office staff, caretakers should all keep this in mind. Above all, a professional manner and common courtesy, in the long run, enhance a school's reputation. Herein lies one of the most important aspects of the principal's leadership.

7.2   The Principal and Public Relations

Forty years ago, the principal could just go ahead and run the school and assume public support. But not today. This is an age of skepticism and those in the public sector seem to receive more than their fair share of questions. Principals must be more public relations conscious. They must keep the public informed.

And the public here encompasses a wide range of people: the parents, the residents near the school, the students, and the staff of neighbouring schools, and the board's administration.

There are many ways to foster good public relations. The following are some suggestions for the principal:

- Encourage staff to phone parents for consultation about student problems, to congratulate them when their child has done well.
- Encourage staff to be careful with hand-outs. Make them easy to read and check the spelling and grammar.
- Make the report cards neat and send them often, at least four per year. Anecdotal cards should be very carefully written.
- Provide each student with a handbook to be taken home. Clearly set forth the school's rules about attendance and deportment.
- Instruct those doing the yearbooks or similar activities about the public relations values of the book and make expectations clear. Do not let the yearbook put down the staff or programs of the school. Make sure educational features are displayed.
- Take a close look at the course calendar. Does it serve the needs and expectations of the community?
- Send out regular newsletters to parents. Distribute them on the same date each month so parents can be sure the student is bringing them home.
- Keep the parents informed about courses and options.
- Run some social events, perhaps a wine and cheese party for staff, or coffee sessions for parents in the afternoons.
- Run an open house from time to time. Consider doing this on a Sunday afternoon, to get more people out.
- Run parents' nights for discussion of children's progress by appointment so parents are not left sitting in the hall for hours. Make these sessions consultations on what parents and teachers as a team can do to help the children succeed.
- Consider a parent-teacher organization of some kind. Make sure that objectives are clear.
- Offer yourself or your interested staff members as speakers at local group meetings: service clubs, religious bodies, town meetings, or public forums.
- Invite representatives of business and industry into the school to discuss what they are looking for in graduates. Let them speak to the young people.
- Write educational and informative articles for the local newspaper. They are usually anxious to receive them.
- Write for educational journals. Do not be afraid to blow the school's horn a bit!
- Write good reports about your school for the board of education or its committees. It is better to involve staff and students before a crisis develops.

- Visit the schools in your area regularly to inform staff and students about your programs. Offer to go right into the classrooms.
- Secondary school principals should keep the feeder schools informed about how their graduates are doing at the secondary school.
- Offer to share equipment within the family of schools.
- Offer to assist the family of schools with professional development programs. Computer education and computer literacy are often of great interest.
- Remember your own staff when dispensing information. Have a good weekly newsletter for staff with lots of facts plus a little humour.
- Follow-up with your own graduates. How are they doing? Did they get the kind of education that was helpful? Relay their reponses back to the staff.
- Keep in touch with colleges and universities. Invite representatives to visit you and take your students to visit them.
- Remember that every time a field trip goes out, the school leaves an impression on the public. The same is true when visitors are invited into the school.
- Proof-read the letters that go out of your school's office. If parents notice one mistake in a suspension letter they ignore the main issues of the problem.

7.3   The Teacher and Public Relations

Teachers must never forget they really work for the public. The representatives of the public—the board of education—may at times seem rather remote. The real public, however, is as near as the next house along the street, and the parents of the students in their classrooms.

To some teachers this is the only public. But there is more to this public. Today the people demand more accountability of all public servants; and they use the media to voice their objections to any shortcomings, whether real or apparent, on the part of teachers. Teachers, therefore, must become more conscious of their own public image and its effect on public relations.

All teachers must recognize that the children are part of the public. It is not enough for the teacher to do a good job of educating the student; the students must feel that they are receiving a good education. Public relations is a part of every classroom and of every lesson.

As the teachers move up in the school, they must take an even broader view of public relations. They must serve the taxpayers. These include not only the parents down the block who are paying property taxes, but also the small and large companies which carry even larger shares of the tax burden. All of society supports education.

Because many truly interested people cannot take the time to visit a school, and a short visit greatly limits what one can see, it is the responsibility of educators to tell the public about education, to tell them of the school's aims and goals, methods, successes and even frustrations. Only then will the public understand the very difficult job of education; only then will they support education.

Exactly who makes up the public? Who has the right and the need to be kept informed? How can an average teacher keep the community informed?

The Students. The aim should be to turn out a satisfied customer. Schools cannot always please the customer, but they must be seen to be working hard and to be well-prepared. The lessons must be useful to each student for the future. Not every course or subject must be job training but every course should be educational. From the moment the teachers drive into the parking lot in the morning until the moment they leave at night, they are communicating with students. Every mood, every smile, every frown has its effect.

The Parents. Some are naturally supportive while some are not. To some the teachers are heroes, to others baby-sitters and overpaid ones at that. If the children are happy in the classroom, then the parent will be supportive. If the children are not successful, if they do not like the teacher, or the subjects, then the parent will be, at the least, suspicious and perhaps even angry. The teachers should use every chance to communicate with the parents in a friendly manner, treating them as important partners in the education of their children. The teachers must not nag or complain; they should be prepared, organized, and objective. At the same time, they must be aware that not all parents are loving toward their children—a call from the teacher could cause problems for the child. If there are any such suspicions, a talk with the guidance office or the principal can prevent misunderstandings.

The following are ways to communicate with parents:
- Use the telephone. (Strangely, some schools do not like teachers to telephone parents.) Early consultation between teacher and parent can head off many problems. Communicate as a concerned person trying to do the best for the student. Do not call over petty things; make the call brief and to the point. Be prepared to offer advice. Be

business-like. Make it clear that you would help after school and suggest help the parent can give, such as monitoring home study. Promise a follow-up call and do call back to report success as well as failure. If you sense major home problems, notify the principal, the guidance office, or both.

— Parents' nights or afternoon interviews are valuable. No matter what process the school uses to set up the appointments, it is a good idea to telephone those you especially want to see and set a definite time for their appointment. If the parent cannot come at that time, arrange your own mutually agreeable schedule. As with telephone interviews, it is important to be prepared. Have all data at hand. If the parent wants to bring the child, welcome both. Nothing is better than all hearing the same words at the same time. Keep good records of these meetings: what was said, what was decided, any follow-up that is necessary. In a personal interview, the teacher is very much under observation; dress and deportment are of great importance. Be business-like.

— All materials handed out to students may be taken home and all of them say a great deal about the teacher. Materials should be neat, spelling should be accurate, grammar should be correct. Photocopied and mimeographed sheets of paper must not be carelessly written or difficult to read. A mature adult may have difficulty making out what is intended; a youngster would find it next to impossible. Poor spelling only confirms that even the teachers cannot spell. Poor editorial style and sloppy phrasing of questions in tests and examinations are examples of very poor public relations. Teachers never know where the products they turn out eventually end up; and they must be careful to turn out a first-class job every time.

— Be sure comments written on tests and examinations are neat and legible. Keep them short and to the point. Watch the spelling and grammar.

— Report cards must be neat and accurate. Comments should be accurate and honest, and hold out some hope for improvement wherever possible. Writing should be legible and certainly free of spelling errors. Remember to say a few kind words wherever possible. Many parents object to computerized, printed remarks; therefore, a personal touch helps take away the institutionalized aspect to some extent.

— If the school has a parent-teacher organization, use it to get to know parents in a comfortable setting. It is one thing to talk about the student's work to the parent, but it is an entirely different thing to get together to discuss education and the needs of the students and the school.

- The teacher who works on any material that goes home to parents, including school newspapers, yearbooks, newsletters and permission forms, should remember that every communication forms part of the image the public has of the school. They should be used to showcase the work of the students and the successes of the school.

The Neighbouring Schools. Those who work there must have a good image of our school. There will be formal times to extend invitations: for example, graduation, orientation, concert, open house. The less formal ones are also good ways simply to become acquainted and to recognize common interests and discuss mutual problems. They are good ways to break down barriers and to dispel suspicions, to develop a community spirit. Sometimes, it is useful to go beyond the feeder schools or family of schools to include staffs from other public, separate or private schools in the area. Schools are all partners in the same business. All serve young people.

Field Trips. These field trips provide excellent opportunities to show the public what students are really like. When teachers plan excursions, they should keep in mind the public relations advantages of the project. The parental permission form sent home by the school is just as significant a piece of public relations as is the subsequent write-up in the school newsletter or the local newspaper. The students' deportment on the bus and at the learning site are two of the best advertisements for education. There is nothing more pleasing and perhaps more surprising to the public than to see a group of young people enjoying themselves, asking pertinent, challenging questions, and learning from the "real" world.

Open House. This involves a lot of work but it can do wonders for the public image of the school. It is best if the students are involved. It is a good opportunity to throw open the doors, invite the public through a notice in the local paper and on the radio. Show the world what a great place the school is.

Music and Drama. Generally, young people love to perform, and parents like to see their children on the stage. Do a thorough job of advertising and put on a good show.

Newspaper Articles. If teachers and principals are willing to take time to write or to have students write informative articles, the local papers will usually run them. All copy should be carefully screened and edited.

Seminars and Workshops. If a currently hot issue is arousing interest, concern or even consternation, why not run a workshop for parents? Such an event might address a particular issue in education or shed light on new directions in education generally. Parents appreciate being informed of new courses; for example, workshops can introduce parents to computers.

7.4   Improving Community Involvement in Education

Speaking at the Community Education Ontario 1977 Conference in Niagara Falls, the Honourable T. L. Wells, then minister of education, defined community involvement in education in the following way:

> Certainly my idea of a community school does include close working relationships between all social agencies which serve a community, ranging from recreation people to social and health workers, as well as educators. These relationships should start with efforts to increase dialogue on a regular basis and lead to better coordination of activities or sharing of facilities. To me, it is integral to the community school that there should be real cooperation between schools and other social agencies which serve a community. More coordination and integration of people-oriented services can be to everyone's advantage. Duplication of effort can be minimized and we can avoid situations where two or more agencies may be trying to help the same people in isolation from each other.

Another approach is more political, that is, it involves people in the community in the decision-making processes of the school. Political activism of this kind reached a peak in the 1970's and has diminished somewhat since; some of the effects remain, however, as shall be examined later.

This community use of schools is not new. In pioneer days, the school was used extensively as a focal point for the community. Often it was the only convenient public hall used for dances, church services, and other public functions. As transportation improved, people travelled more easily to specialized facilities, so the use of the local school building diminished. Giles (1978) states, however, that in the 1960's and 1970's, interest in adult education developed. Because the most suitable facilities for these programs were the high school buildings, the school once again became a centre for community activities. This renewed interest frequently presented problems for principals, teachers and the school board, for the modern school is far more complex, with much expensive apparatus. This frequently created a conflict between the interests of the school and those of the public over the use (and abuse) of equipment and facilities. Gradually, policies were worked out so that the community could make much greater use of what they considered to be "their" schools. Trustees are, after all, politicians who soon felt the direction in which the wind was blowing.

To promote the community use of schools, a select committee of the Ontario Legislature was established in 1971. It examined the use of school facilities throughout Ontario. The committee heard presentations and visited schools throughout the province as well as in the United Kingdom, Scandinavia, the Netherlands, and the United States. The committee decided that more was needed than the mere development of the mechanics of community use of schools. The community must also participate in deciding how to use and develop the local facilities. Some key recommendations in the final report included:

- The minister of education should instruct school boards to encourage public participation in the designing and rehabilitation of schools.
- The procedures to sell or lease a school should be changed to allow for a greater community involvement in the decision.
- School boards should no longer charge fees for community use of their facilities.
- The minister of education should incorporate into the Education Act the principle that access to schools as community facilities is a right, not just a privilege.
- The ministry of community and social services, in consultation with the minister of education, should institute a program for supervised care and recreation of elementary school children before and after school and during the lunch period.

A school or board can develop a community school approach in the following ways:

- Programs that encourage individuals or groups to use their schools.
- Programs that encourage the school to use community resources.
- The use of adult volunteers in the classroom and elsewhere.
- The establishment of a school-community advisory committee.
- A community-school coordinator.

Margaret Gayfer's booklet, *Open Doors,* commissioned by the ministry of education in 1976, describes in some detail such programs. Any could serve as models for such a scheme.

In the future, facilities may be consolidated further to save on some of the obvious items—heating, parking, maintenance and security. This is not always easy to do in some provinces. Local governments in Ontario, for example, have four corporate bodies with jurisdiction in community education. The public board of education, the separate school board, the municipal council (operating mainly through the parks and recreation department), and the public library board—all have an interest in educational or recreational activities. Joint use has been established in some cases (notably swimming facilities), but much still needs to be done.

Community participation in decisions reached a peak in the mid-1970's, with parents and others securing certain rights to decide on activities and even to recommend the appointments of principals. This idea does exist elsewhere; for example, in England and Wales the boards of governors (secondary schools) and managers (elementary schools) have operated for some time. These are made up of local councillors (there are no boards of education, as such), citizens, and in some cases, teachers and pupils. Their powers are limited, but the principle of local participation applies.

In Ontario, such practices are not widespread, confined mainly to "alternative" schools within the publicly-supported school systems. The more notable achievements include greater provision of French-language classes, and special education and heritage language programs. In all these cases, the boards of education either lobbied the ministry of education or else instituted programs as far as they were legally permitted to do.

In the early 1970's, groups sought to participate in the administration of schools, notably in the appointment of principals. In a few cases, panels representing various interest groups were actually established; by-and-large, however, this movement died a natural death in most areas.

It is interesting to note that one of the most important functions of the boards of managers or governors in the United Kingdom is the recommending of a new head-teacher to the education committee. This advice is usually followed. In Ontario, the methods of closing schools, coupled with strict holding back of expenses (a common theme among candidates for election in 1982) steered community interest away from more direct intervention. The possible advent of party politics may have an effect. The New Democratic Party ran candidates in 1982, with varying degrees of success. In the city of Toronto, the party forms a large caucus and thus brings pressure upon the government of Ontario. This could affect community involvement in decision-making as well as the provision of more facilities for community use of schools.

7.5   Volunteer Help in the School

The contemporary use of the word "volunteer" brings to mind adult lay people who help teachers in the classroom on an unpaid basis. Before, voluntary help was usually associated with special events such as field trips or raising money. Frequently, the home and school or parent-teacher association supplemented the work of teachers. The "enriched school lunch program" is one of the most significant services instituted by parent volunteers. Not only do these mothers plan, purchase, prepare and serve nutritious inexpensive meals to students, but they often also assume responsibility for noon hour supervision and for financial reports to the administration. These programs in inner city schools are usually partially supported by the board and tend to be managed by a volunteer school and community committee.

More recently, some schools have used volunteers to help in various tasks under the direction of the principal or a professional teacher. They have become a valuable, if not widespread, addition to the hierarchy of teaching. The presence of such people eventually raised the question of legal liability. An amendment to the Education Act in the 1970's legitimized the position of the voluntary assistant.

The motives of these volunteers are many. Many, largely the women, volunteer out of a sense of civic duty. Some use the experience to upgrade skills, others to acquire skills in a new field, yet others to test themselves before starting a new career. Retired people volunteer for the pleasure of an outside interest. The benefits of a grandmotherly or grandfatherly image in the school can be substantial.

In all cases for volunteers, regardless of motive, the teacher and the principal have two important administrative tasks: selecting suitable people, and seeing that they receive adequate training. They have to interview the volunteers carefully; volunteers, after all, are making a commitment to the school. Both the principal and staff must know exactly what skills they can bring to the classroom, what time they can spare and what is their commitment. To prevent any misunderstandings, it is essential to explain carefully the respective roles of the teachers and the volunteers. The volunteers must understand the school policies and procedures, the need for confidentiality and reliability, and the ways to deal with many children at one time.

7.6   Lobbies

The school and the school board are frequently the targets of people with vested interest. These groups may be small, or represent a national organization; their objectives may be educational, religious, political, ecological, or personal. Boards of education commonly prepare policies to deal with such activities; it is the principal's duty to see that the staff are well aware of them in order to avoid embarrassing occasions. If there is no policy, it would be wise to discuss the requests with a responsible official or a trustee, to find out if there are any counter forces in the district who might reasonably object, or inform others what is being done. Public education is just that: the rights of the majority and the minority should both be respected, especially when all contribute towards the funding of schools.

All this poses a difficult dilemma for the professional in a bureaucracy. Principals and staff must be fully aware of the community and the groups within it. Principals should avoid conflict with lobbies. Frequently, these can be called upon for help — the wise principal will establish contact with as many such groups as is possible.

Parents may also form groups to lobby for lunch-hour supervision with or without a lunch program, for example. In these cases, the principal can work with the board and the group for the best possible arrangement. Or, in the case of groups seeking traffic lights, crossing guards or stop-signs, for example, the principal might even intervene and support a specific proposal. At all times, when considering the requests of such groups, the principals and staff must keep the best interests of the pupils and the community in mind, taking into account any policies the board may have. Here is another chance for good public relations.

8 Values

8 Values

8.1 Values: Public, Separate, Alternative, and Private/Independent Schools

The universal declaration of human rights (Section III, Paragraph 26) states categorically that parents have the right to decide the kind of education they want for their children. Educational policy-makers in Canada strive toward that ideal, hence the wide variety of schools across Canada. Parents can choose among public, separate and alternative schools supported by tax rates, as well as private and independent schools supported by fees, foundations, or private funding.

The public system may be likened to a political party in power which has a responsibility as "the government for all the people." It is just as impossible for a school system to be neutral or value-free as it is for a political party to so propose itself. But the communitarian values of the public school system do not fully take into account those of all the communities, whether religious, ethnic, or social.

Values are persisting beliefs or preferences that influence the choice of behaviour. Internalized values guide behaviour and attitudes towards persons, objects, and situations. As standards, values serve three purposes:

- To justify (that is, make coherent) one's attitudes and actions as well as those of others
- To make judgements about oneself and others, as well as to compare oneself to others
- To influence the values, attitudes and activities of others, such as students

When persons face conflicting role expectations, their decisions depend not only on their own values but also on how strongly they hold them. Values affect action and help one to determine whether goals are means or ends (Sheehan, 1972). Most educators can agree on the means of education; they often do not agree about the ends.

One popular idea is that the end of education is to make economically useful citizens. Of course, the essence of education is first to prepare the best possible citizens. It is foolish to separate education for the person from education for the economic commonweal. The commonweal depends on well-educated people; and a good education is impossible without a healthy commonweal. The citizen needs a network of social ties where there is an understanding of community and of the virtues needed for relating to the community.

There is usually a general agreement on the means of education. Standards of teacher certification, required days of instruction, base curriculum, modes of evaluation and promotion, and lawful disciplinary measures, are common throughout public, separate, alternative and independent/private schools. The systems differ about the ends of education, the diversity of value systems.

Public schools institutionalize a public philosophy and foster broadly acceptable values. These affect the administration of schools. An abiding concern to be neutral about religious values, so much so that teachers do not freely express their own values, may lead to a slightly artificial condition where the lowest common denominator is the norm. Public schools also tend to mirror rather than criticize the society they serve. They emphasize the goals of society in the present or immediate future. Historic reference is largely confined to civic realities, the nation-state, the geographic community.

Although religious schools must likewise come to terms with the current political conditions, they also act as a centre for a specific concept of the world, of man, and of history. This also affects administration. But within it, there is a strong commitment to family and community. It has a psychological foundation based on shared religious belief. It emphasizes a respect for spiritual realities, above all, the evolving dynamism of each student's self-appropriation of truth. The teachers' enthusiasm and reverence inspire learning, without submerging the private self or values. Moreover, their personal convictions and passions point to a personhood fully realized. Being in the community and of it, such teachers may affirm its goodness or speak out against its evil. They introduce students to a religious tradition that transcends immediate political or geographic entities.

No simple separation between public and religious systems is possible. Among tax-based schools, the public system (formerly undifferentiatedly Christian and now increasingly neutral) and the separate system (almost uniformly Catholic but increasingly less sectarian given the character of post-Vatican II Catholicism) are both to varying degrees religious. Of non-tax-based systems, the independent/private schools are not all religious. In private Catholic schools, the values associated with social, athletic or academic achievement may sometimes counter-balance religious values. Catholics are very serious about religious values permeating their schools. Ontario Separate School trustees (1974) state:

> In a religious school for Catholic adolescents, the students should be a dynamic segment of a living Christian community: naturally teachers are expected to contribute to the vitality of this religious community. Their own living and lived faith will inspire the miracle of its growth in the students.

An instruction from the Vatican secretariat for education (S.C.C.E., 1977) in Rome asserts that "complete education includes a religious dimension" but the school is also a "place of integral formation" where students grow into a Christian culture through gradual, purposeful and critical assimilation.

This type of education demands much more than mere catechetical instruction in "released time" or a Sunday-school approach.

> In helping pupils to achieve through the medium of its teaching an integration of faith and culture, the Catholic School sets out with a deep awareness of the value of knowledge as such. Under no circumstances does it wish to divert the imparting of knowledge from its rightful objective. Individual subjects must be taught according to their own particular methods (S.C.C.E., 1977).

Because of their diverse constituencies, public schools cannot respond to the Catholic community's demand for such integral formation. They cannot concern themselves with "living and lived faith" or encourage their students to be a "dynamic segment of a living Christian community." The public school must conform to a standard administrative and political abstraction not in touch with sections of the community. Because of their homogeneous constituencies, religious schools enjoy much support. *Inner City, Private Education: A Study* (1982) makes this point:

> The inner city private schools [that is, schools in the United States] have been able to flourish with the sharply decentralized authority structure, partly because of the strong bonds of consensus linking the teachers, administrators, parishes and parents.

In these inner-city private schools, the role of the principal is substantially different from the principals in the public schools. In the private schools they are not burdened by layers of administration and bureaucracy. They can take a far more active and intimate role in the daily operation of the school and can work on a daily basis with teachers and students. They usually know each student and their families personally.

A recent review of *High School Achievement: Public, Catholic and Private Schools Compared* (1982) in the *New Leader* (Nov. 27, 1982) makes some interesting observations:

> There is reason to think that, besides disciplining their students more rigorously, private schools nurture them better. Some quantitative evidence in the book supports for every 323 students the ratio in Catholic Schools is 1:235; in non-Catholic private schools, it is 1:55. Public schools, moreover have one volunteer for every 839 pupils; Catholic schools have one per 385, and other private schools one per 101. Although scarcely surprising, given that non-public institutions must have active support to survive, this statistic indicates how much greater their level of familial and community commitment is.

The wider the target of a social organization, the more generalized is the group it addresses. And it is less responsive to individuals, families, or elements of the community. The social organization becomes a large body. Its movements are awkward, less able to work with the smallest elements it serves as if from greater distance. Some students simply do not do well in schools well designed for most of their peers.

Thus, the diversity and plurality of different learning styles have created a need for alternative schools different from conventional schools and even different from each other. *A Brief Look at Public Alternative Schools in Ontario* (Freedman *et al.,* 1980) says of them:

> Most alternative schools begin with the notion that they can remedy a large number of conventional inadequacies. One school was begun in response to a drop-out problem within its board. What appeared as a single problem turned out to be a set of problems.

Canadian educational policy differs from province to province. But part of its genius lies in allowing freedom to choose from a diversity of educational experiences, different kinds of schools supported by the public taxes. It is, however, not as broad as the ideal of the UNESCO Declaration of Human Rights. It is unclear whether some implicit social contract is its philosophical foundation; what is true is that a constitutional contract with respect to our bilingual, bicultural origins results in our present pluralism. E. L. Edmonds, "In Defence of the Private School" (Education Canada, 1981), asserts this:

> The separate school system offers an alternative form of education, which pertains today in five out of the ten provinces of Canada. The alternative school system as it operates in, say British Columbia or Ontario, has been widely acclaimed. It is one reason, among others, why I think we in Canada are the most democratic citizens of the world.

Canada and the United States may share many social myths but they also have quite different sets of values. Arnold Toynbee once remarked on the danger attendant upon the American view of schools as agents of cultural assimilation: he sees the pledge of allegiance ceremony that begins the American public school day as a rite of restrictionist or national religion. Similarly, Donald A. Erickson wrote (in Inner City, 1982):

> It is discouraging that educational research, a purportedly scientific endeavour, is still so biased and distorted by loyalty to any established institution (the public school).

It is a tribute to Canadian education that our schools represent an established pluralism. Diverse systems of values prevail. To be sure, tensions do exist but there is also a climate, an improving climate, of freedom of choice.

This established pluralism is not merely for the good of the independent communities it addresses. Interdependent values also serve the good of the whole larger community. Cooperation in musical, athletic and theatrical programs are examples of this.

But a specific instance of cooperative curricular development illustrates the pluralism described here. In 1960, after the launching of Sputnik, the Toronto Board of Education at the University of Toronto initiated a study of the teaching of English, science and the social studies. This research developed into the Ontario Curriculum Institute, which focused the efforts of different levels and systems in the educational world as well as the work of some remarkably dedicated teachers.

The Science Committee, which came to be situated in an independent school, provides a fascinating example of the many benefits of pluralism in education. Its history speaks to the desirability of having instructors of venerable age who stand over against the Establishment, and whose judgement tests the authenticity of causes and whose independence can sustain a good cause till it comes of age (Sheehan, 1977).

The account of this case study stands as an effective paradigm of inter-related values systems operative among public, separate and independent schools.

8.2   The Teacher as Values Educator

Values Education is not a subject. It is a theme, a unifying principle of action, the sum total of pedagogical choices. In every subject, a teacher leads students to think, judge and act. Values in a classroom can be recognized by examining decisions that are consistently made in that classroom.

In some sense, the process of valuing is like that of learning with its empirical, rational and responsible dimensions. The empirical or affective dimension includes sensing, perceiving, imagining, feeling, speaking and moving—the basis for likes and dislikes. The rational or cognitive dimension includes such activities as enquiry, understanding, expression, analysis, reflection, comparison, and judgement (true/false, certain/probable). The responsible or cognitive dimension includes the ability to deliberate, evaluate, decide and act. Thus, values formation includes a rational cognition, a centring affection and an organizing love or will (Lonergan, 1972).

When the affective and cognitive dimensions speak with one voice, the values decisions are harmonious. When a decision is based on self-chosen principles and not on compliance with borrowed moral rules, it is identified with the person and engages personal responsibility. Peters (1981) states that to be operative in one's conduct, the principles must be accepted as one's own; the principles actually move the person to act.

Values education therefore is not simply the skill of applying timeless moral principles to a series of moral dilemmas; it is the art of responding to the tasks of everyday life in and out of the classroom by actions that are truly humanizing and liberating. "Seeing" then will determine "doing." Teachers with this conviction can help their students to find coherence and meaning in their lives. Values are intrinsic to justice, responsibility, caring, and love. Freedom from selfish concern becomes the key to responsible living.

The aim of values education is autonomy—freedom to make independent decisions with confidence, not influenced by emotional reactions, social pressures, or conditioning. This does not mean a denial of customs and norms, the accumulation of the best of human thought and experience. It does mean that teachers encourage their students to examine options, to consider consequences, and then to act courageously according to principle.

The teacher's task in values education can be summed up in three key strategies: build a world; nurture a life; and awaken a spirit.

Build a World. This task is akin to construction with materials chosen for their durability, strength, suitability, and bonding qualities. The teacher creates an environment where the student learns to learn; the student recognizes inappropriate behaviour by the same self-evaluation that Montessori built into her learning materials. The classroom should mirror reality, and the program should include opportunities for practice. The arrangement of physical space can teach concepts of security, safety, and beauty. Sharing space can promote principles of cooperation and collaboration.

In building the student's world, the teachers can exemplify

Honesty—by teaching respect for work, materials and rights of others.

Open-mindedness—by offering alternatives in choice of media, methods, activities, and assignments.

Willingness—by offering advantages to their students, which may mean "going the extra mile."

Nurture a Life. The values educator is concerned both with the externals of the student's program and the student as an organism. Students are like plants—they need space, light, water, warmth and time.
- *Space.* The teacher provides room for students to grow, to learn, to become who they are. What students see and what teachers see form only a part of what the student is. When the teacher recognizes the child's space, belongings, and work, the child learns to respect the property of others. The Montessori mat illustrates this kind of incidental values education. Orderly procedures, careful storage, and handling of classroom equipment further reinforce this respect.
- *Light.* The teacher's experience can be light for the student. Sharing personal wisdom and insights illuminates the students' reflections about their own experiences— "This worked for me." Here the teacher needs a passion for patience in order not to preach or push. This is the lovely art of leaving things alone.

— *Water*. Into every life a little rain must fall. To recognize the total person, the teacher does not have to know everything, but to understand. Allowance must be made for emotional expression. The teacher can show ways to deal with anger, resentment, joy, success. To be responsible, the student must be free to choose a response. How teachers themselves express or control their own feelings will reinforce their teaching.

— *Warmth*. The climate in a classroom affects the growth of students. They blossom in an atmosphere of joy and encouragement. In a classroom, unreasonable demands produce anxiety. When the teacher provides *super*vision, evaluation and even correction can be helpful. Rules that are clear, consistent, fair and reasonable, promote confidence and contentment in spite of limitations.

— *Time*. This implies care and concern, personal presence. Respect is the base of all growth for the teacher, the student, and the community. The teacher can plan to "touch" each student individually. These contacts can be subtly built into daily lesson plans and classroom procedures. These investments cost no money and pay large dividends.

Awaken a Spirit. Students not only have an innate ability to grow, but are also self-determining. The third task of the values educator, therefore, is to inspire. Students are persons — autonomous and unique. They can always be more competent, more skilful, more accurate, and more responsive. The teachers' task here involves stimulating, motivating, setting goals, challenging, and providing clear expectations, sound models, high standards, and frequent responses for their reflection. The teacher must listen.

It is just as important for teachers to listen to what the students are not saying. Language conveys thoughts as well as feelings. But there are also non-verbal language and messages. To make sure the words and music go together, the teachers must learn to paraphrase, to check perceptions, to play back the tape. They must listen to the reason and then listen for the real reason. Dr. Edward Rosen, a child psychologist, used to repeat the following phrase over and over again to his graduate students: "That's what the patient is saying but what is he telling you?"

This kind of values education in a classroom requires careful and thoughtful management. The teacher must encourage creative and divergent thought, long-range thinking and action planning. Conflict is a part of a dynamic organism. Manageable, productive team-work can lead to greater congruence between the norms and goals of individual students and those of the class and school. Happy students learn and grow.

Teachers must know and care for their students, understand motivational theory to challenge and sustain a climate of trust and openness, and develop a collegial approach to problem-solving and decision-making in their classrooms. Teachers who know their students and respect the law (the Education Act, the ministry regulations and policies, the board's policies and procedures, the school's rules and expectations) can teach students the benefits of law and promote the attitudes necessary to live freely within the law. Only a free person can choose to obey.

Good teachers believe that each student is a unique creation, that each one reflects a unique expression of Beauty, Truth and Goodness, that each one has a unique contribution to make to our world.

They accept the challenge to discover and reveal this unique gift, to encourage its development, and to provide the tools for the task. Advice for aspiring administrators applies equally to prospective values educators: "Point the way; lead the way; and then get yourself out of the way."

8.3 The Teacher as Philosopher

Just as the school is a privileged place where growth is fostered by means of a systematic and critical assimilation of culture, the teacher is also a privileged person who provides a living encounter with a cultural heritage through personal contact and commitment.

Teachers spend about thirty hours a week as the primary supervisors of children's learning and socialization. The teacher's view of reality or attitude to life enters into every decision in a school. The teacher's *perception* of society—the community, the nation, the world and the *value* placed on the relationship between the student and these communal realities—is significant for the development of students. It matters, for instance, whether the teacher sees the child as a unit in a collective, or as a radically discrete individual, or as a person whose rights are related to but perhaps also divergent from the common good of society.

According to Jacques Maritain (1952), "The right of a child to be educated requires that the educator shall have moral authority over him, and this authority is nothing else than the duty of the adult to the freedom of the youth." In the final analysis, the authority of the teacher to educate determines the understanding of truth and adherence to values. The teacher's personal success in living an examined life enhances this authority. Only such teachers can answer the needs of students in a society with depersonalization, mass production, and manipulative propaganda. Only such teachers can develop persons who are inner-directed, able to make free and responsible choices. Only those who know what learning is, and what its purposes are, are free from pressures of immediate utility, of fashion and fad. These teachers are open to the full array of human and social values.

This is not an easy job. No teacher has anything like absolute authority. Without claiming perfection — in fact, by admitting to imperfections — real teachers progress towards inner authority. The classroom becomes a place that initiates a fascination with learning and the first steps to ultimate truth and values.

As philosophical perception establishes authority in any classroom, it has greater significance in today's multicultural society.

8.4　The Teacher as Global Educator

Robert Hanvey (1974) points out the necessity for the teacher today to adopt a "global perspective." But a global perspective is not enough. The teacher must also adopt a global agenda for the classroom. The technological electronic revolution, with its mass media and mass phenomena, has opened a new age of world community — an ecological age.

Teachers today have the privilege of introducing their students into a totally new era of interdependencies, fashioned both by nature and by people, and revealed by science as a web of life and eco-systems and cycles. As they learn for themselves, they must also teach their students to use constructively a new social environment, the product of the silicon chip and the microprocessor. At the same time, they must anticipate how the microcomputer and macroprocesses will affect the students, the curriculum, and the goals of education.

What is the impact of this new knowledge and technology on teaching? In the past, maintenance learning was all that was necessary. The teacher passed on the wisdom of the past and the cultural heritage of parents and society, and prepared students for a predictable future in familiar jobs supported by relatively stable social institutions. The teacher now, however, must deal with

> such dramatically changed circumstances which deeply affect our lives, there is an urgent need for more global education. This is very important for the future of humankind. How can our children go to school and learn so much detail about the past, the geography and the administration of their country and so little about the world, its global problems, its interdependencies, its future, and its international institutions? ... A child born today will be faced as an adult, almost daily, with problems of a global interdependent nature.... He will be both an actor and a beneficiary or a victim in the total world fabric, and he may rightly ask: "Why was I not warned? Why was I not better educated?" (Muller, n.d.).

Maintenance learning has to be replaced by innovative learning. In what McLuhan called our Electronic Surround, the teacher must develop the planet's greatest resource: "the valuable deposits of 'gray matter' in the heads of young and old learners alike" (Shane, 1982). With the microchip, the teacher can help create what Brown (1981) terms a "sustainable society." Students must learn to think globally while acting locally because the inhabitants of a wired planet will survive together or not at all. The world needs the resources of everyone.

Robert Hanvey (1979) lists five dimensions to a world view necessary for a pedagogical philosophy.
- *Perspective consciousness* recognizes that others have views of the world that are profoundly different from our own.
- *State-of-the-planet-awareness* is basic knowledge about prevailing world conditions and developments in the social and ecological environment of the global village.
- *Cross-cultural-awareness* looks at the students' culture from the perspective of others and the ability to relate effectively to individuals and groups of other ethnic origins.
- *Knowledge of global dynamics* recognizes the inter-active relations of cultural entities as systems.
- *Awareness of human choices* recognizes how teachers and students may participate in global systems.

To develop a personal philosophy of education, the teachers should follow the six conditions for effective teaching as set out in *The Professional Education of Teachers* (Combs *et al.,* 1974):
- Knowledge of the world and of their subjects.
- Sensitivity to people, the capacity for empathy.
- Accurate and appropriate beliefs about people and their behaviour.
- Favourable beliefs about self.
- Appropriate and congruent beliefs about purposes, the goals of society, schools, the classroom and the teachers' own goals of teaching.
- The personal discovery of their own appropriate and authentic ways of teaching.

To avoid having students conceive of the future world community as a type of "Big Brother" world government, two principles should be taught:
- *Consensus:* agreement by negotiation rather than by win/lose vote.
- *Subsidiarity:* decision and action at the lowest possible level of involvement and implementation. A global public sector or a global institution is needed only where the issue is global; for example, environment, disarmament, and where the effects are felt globally rather than only nationally.

In global education, the teaching space is a model (microcosm) of the world (macrocosm). Full advantage should be taken of the prolific global data provided by the United Nations.

The UN has issued documents through *UNESCO: Recommendation Concerning Education for International Understanding, Cooperation and Peace and Education Relating to Human Rights and Fundamental Freedoms. (1974).* These documents should be used not only by teachers but also by staff and student-teachers in faculties of education. The following excerpts provide guiding principles for a global agenda:

> Education should be infused with the aims and purposes set forth in the Charter of the United Nations, the Constitution of Unesco and the *Universal Declaration of Human Rights* (1974) particularly *Article 26, paragraph 2*, of the last-named, which states: "Education shall be directed to the full development of the human personality and to the strengthening of respect for human rights and fundamental freedoms. It shall promote understanding, tolerance and friendship among all nations, racial or religious groups, and shall further the activities of the United Nations for the maintenance of peace."

9 Professionalism in Practice

9 Professionalism in Practice

9.1 Professional Organizations

The meaning of the term "professional" in the abstract was discussed in an earlier chapter. Below are organizations to which Ontario teachers belong, whether by choice or by statute. These include:

- Ontario Teachers' Federation (O.T.F.) with its five affiliates (OSSTF), (FWTAO), (OPSTF), (OECTA), (AEFO)
- Canadian Teachers' Federation (C.T.F.)
- Canadian Education Association (C.E.A.)
- Canadian Society for the Study of Education (C.S.S.E.)
- Ontario Association of Education Administrative Officials (OAEAO)

Information about these organizations can be obtained in booklet form at the O.T.F. office, 1260 Bay Street, Toronto. Teachers should also study the Teaching Profession Act passed in 1944.

The teachers' federations deal with the general welfare of teachers (including salaries and working conditions), as well as the broader issues (for example, the self-licensing concept for teachers, new certification requirements, and curriculum guidelines). Other organizations cater to more specialized needs. Teachers should take part in at least one other professional association besides their federation.

The most important organization for the principals is the teachers' federation. Principals belong to the same professional organization, to the same union, as their subordinates. There are few other jobs where the manager belongs to the same trade union as the employee. This can cause confusion and problems.

In some parts of the world, the principal may not have been a teacher but may come into administration by way of business administration courses. But in Ontario, for example, the principal is the "principal teacher." The Education Act defines the principal's duties as follows: "It is the duty of a principal of a school, in addition to his duties as a teacher, to ..." Clearly, the principal is expected to hold teaching qualifications. Every principal went through a teachers' college or faculty of education and holds a teaching certificate. The principal's qualifications are obtained later by taking other courses.

In Ontario every teacher is automatically considered to be a member of a teachers' federation upon graduation and obtaining a contract. Thus, the principal is a member of the teachers' federation as a teacher; and this membership is maintained when the person becomes a principal. For example, the Ontario Secondary School Teachers' Federation (O.S.S.T.F.) has a division called the Ontario Secondary School Headmasters' Council (O.S.S.H.C.) to which principals belong. This is an extra affiliation for principals. They are still members of the parent federation — O.S.S.T.F.

Principals were among the founders of the federations. For years, they were among its strongest members. When teachers were a little afraid to speak out, the principals spoke out for them and initiated many of the improvements that have come to teachers over the years. Unfortunately, in recent times, the federation seems to have become more militant, perhaps out of necessity, and has taken on more the action and appearance of a trade union. Certain members, being trade union conscious, ignored the advantages of having middle management people, the principals, in the organization. They put much pressure on principals. There has even been some talk of the principals getting out of federation and joining the superintendents in separate professional organizations. Fortunately, this idea has greatly diminished recently. The principals still have their problems but level heads on both sides point to the advantages of keeping principals in the federation. To prevent discord, all members should keep the following in mind.

Principals were and are teachers. Many still teach.

Principals are in middle management positions, not unlike a branch manager in a large organization. They have certain responsibilities different from those of teachers. At times, these may put them in conflict with a few teachers. They have to evaluate teachers. Sometimes, they have to insist that teachers do a better job or even fire teachers. This is a difficult position but surely one that both sides can understand.

In disputes between teacher and principal, the federation must not seem to be taking sides, but rather must act as mediator to ensure that the proper process has been followed. With their great experience in such matters, the federation officers should advise both the principal and the teacher. The desire to give the teacher a little more protection is natural —

to protect the underling from the manager. It should always be clear, however, that the federation is in the middle. It represents both parties and so must give honest and fair advice to both. It is not easy for the teacher or the principal, or the federation.

The interests of the principal are somewhat different from those of the average teacher. This is natural and should not become a point of division between teachers and principals. It is quite possible to have two sets of interests and responsibilities. Instead of pressuring the principal, the federation should offer sensible advice that recognizes the nature of the principal's position. The following are a few examples: If there is a strike, the School Boards and Teachers Collective Negotiations Act in Ontario separates the principal from the teachers. It requires principals to stay in the schools to do whatever must be done for the safety of the students and the plant. This is the law. The federation should not urge the principal to break that law. The principals may be separated from the staff by location—the one inside the building the rest outside—but this does not mean they are separated in their principles or in their aspirations or demands. Some principals will be morally opposed to strikes just as some teachers will be; this has nothing to do with what each must do under the law in a certain situation.

At contract negotiations, the interests of principals are somewhat different from those of staff. Salaries are different, and managing the demands of the contract is more a burden for the principal than for the teacher. The federation would be wise to support as high as possible salaries for principals: the higher the principal's salary, the more it will pull the staff salaries along with it. If possible, the principals should have a representative on the direct negotiations team, not just on the salary committee. The federations should always ask for advice from the principals about management items they are trying to introduce into the contract. The federations should avoid items in the contract that are hard to manage or items that favour teachers over principals and vice-principals. For example, a clause that states quite specifically what teachers must teach, allowing no exceptions, makes it impossible for any teacher to be given time for administrative experience in the office. That is not good for the teacher who wants the experience, or for the principal and vice-principal who need help.

The interests of principals differ from those of teachers in other ways. These should not be used to divide; instead, they can bring the two groups together, to understand the other's positions and to assist each other for mutual benefit. Having a manager who is still very much a part of the team is an advantage.

9.2   Teachers and Collective Bargaining

One significant task of the professional association is the annual negotiations. As described by Myers (1973), collective bargaining is a process engaged in by representatives of the employer and of the employees. They meet at mutually convenient times to discuss, in good faith, conditions of employment, including salary, conditions of work, fringe benefits and other items. Their goal is to draw up a contract incorporating any agreement reached by the two parties. Bargaining in good faith means that both parties consider each other's viewpoint when presenting proposals and that outrageous demands are not made. Agreement is not necessarily part of the process, nor is the making of concessions.

For many years, the items were almost entirely concerned with salary and a few fringe benefits. Over the years, sabbatical leave, retirement plans and various leave-of-absence conditions were negotiated, but basic salaries and allowances for responsibility were the major points at issue. Before the early 1970's, the school boards could legally make unilateral decisions. They were not bound to negotiate at all. Most did, but the possible sanctions held by teachers were not clear cut.

Most negotiations were carried out in a friendly "gentlemanly" way. A group of teachers elected at the local level met from time to time with the board and eventually hammered out an agreement. Each side came armed with statistics on the cost-of-living and salaries for comparable positions in other school boards or other professions. By-and-large, there was a spirit of compromise. But changes were on the way, brought on by increasing militancy among teachers. In the 1960's, teachers began hearing of industrial-type methods in New York and elsewhere. Moreover, the vast influx of teachers with industrial experience exerted an increasing influence upon the federation. In 1967-8 there were pink-listings and the Ontario School Trustees' Council even organized a moratorium on hiring. The federation followed with threats of mass resignations in metropolitan Toronto. This tactic was again used in 1970, when hiring was delayed until June from the traditional March date.

One significant change in negotiations was the addition of working conditions. This item often took priority over salary matters. It was becoming clear that the federations were not only including additional items to negotiate, but also seeking a share in determining the day-to-day operations in schools. Perhaps this ambition was not widely recognized by members; with hindsight, however, one sees in it some of the origins of today's collective bargaining procedures.

The conflicts began to increase in length and bitterness through the early 1970's (Downie, 1978). In 1973 and 1974, several serious conflicts occurred during negotiations. Mass resignations actually went through in three boards. The spending ceilings imposed by the provincial government in 1971-2 had exacerbated the situation. The government was drawn in in early 1973 when it settled the disputes in two cases by conciliation processes and the third, by arbitration. By the end of 1973, more mass resignations caused the government to legislate teachers back to work by declaring their resignations void, or at least postponed for a further month. In the meantime, the government prepared more permanent legislation. In December 1973, about 30,000 teachers staged a mass rally at the legislature.

Most disputes were eventually settled by arbitration or otherwise, and the government relaxed the ceilings on spending to facilitate the process.

"Bill 100." The School Boards and Teachers Collective Negotiations Act (or Bill 100) received royal assent on July 18, 1975. This act gave teachers the right to bargain collectively for conditions of employment, fringe benefits and salary, as well as the right to strike.

The act incorporates some interesting and novel approaches. A permanent body, the Education Relations Commission, assists the boards and teachers. In addition, under certain conditions, a "fact-finder" can be appointed to study both sides of a dispute. Other parts of the act deal with strikes and lockouts, arbitration, final offer selection, and details of negotiating procedures.

Negotiating Procedures. Negotiations between the parties begin within 30 days of notice being served in January by either party. If there is no quick agreement, the parties may take one of three steps:
- Request the Commission to assign a person to assist the parties to make or renew the agreement
- Request the Commission to appoint a fact-finder
- Refer all matters in the dispute between them that may be provided for in an agreement to an arbitrator or a board of arbitration or a selector for determination

If the first is chosen, then an agreement may be reached or another method may follow; if an arbitrator or selector, then an agreement is reached; if a fact-finder, then the report is made public. But if no agreement follows, then a secret ballot is held by teachers on whether to strike; and final offer selection or voluntary arbitration or further bargaining may take place.

If these occur as a result of the vote, then an agreement is reached. If, however, the teachers decide, by secret ballot, to hold a strike, then a legal strike can be called for September 1st at the earliest; that is, seven months after notice of negotiations had been given on January 1st.

The Education Relations Commission (ERC). The Lieutenant Governor in Council appoints the five members of the Education Relations Commission. Normally, they are persons with expertise in educational affairs who are seen to be impartial. The ERC oversees many details of the negotiating process, and trains and appoints mediators, fact-finders, and arbitrators. In a prolonged strike, the ERC makes recommendations to the minister based on the perceived effects of the strike on the students.

Fact-finder. When the ERC decides that negotiations between teachers and board are at an impasse, it may appoint a fact-finder to study the case. The fact-finder may recommend terms for settlement, but these are not binding upon either party. The fact-finder's report is made public after fifteen days. Then public opinion may persuade one or both parties to suggest changes or agreement.

Arbitration. Both parties may agree to voluntary binding arbitration — over all or part of the agreement in question. They may agree on an arbitrator or may request the ERC to supply one. The decision of the arbitrator is binding upon both parties.

Final-offer Selection. This approach is like arbitration but differs in one important aspect: an arbitrator can choose among options from either side or steer a course between them; a final-offer selector must choose all of one or all of the other package. The idea behind this second approach is that parties to a dispute will hesitate to take too extreme a position lest their list be rejected in favor of one that is more moderate.

Strikes and Lock-outs. A strike includes not only a concerted refusal to be present in the school but also work-to-rule and notice of group resignation. In a lock-out, the board suspends teachers (but not principals and vice-principals) or refuses to assign work to them. While teachers are on strike or locked out, they are not paid.

Strike procedures have different effects on boards and teachers. Strikes give the boards some idea of the strength of the teachers' feelings when the results of the strike vote are made public. They can seek to have a strike declared illegal before the Ontario Labour Relations Board. They can also lock teachers out if they choose (with due regard to political results), under certain conditions.

Teachers have the advantage of deciding when strike votes will be taken and what sanctions will be applied. They are also able to rally support at times that are best suited to them.

In the long run, both sides are under pressure from the public and frequently from the pupils. They often make decisions to accommodate the political realities. Indeed, in viewing the progress of a strike and making recommendations to the minister, the ERC must take into account political as well as educational factors. Certainly the government must do so.

Teachers' organizations have found the current system, generally speaking, to their liking. Trustees and senior administrators would not agree. The important role of fact-finder has probably helped solve many disputes. According to Downie (1978), the main complaint is that negotiations tend to be drawn out and to spill over well into the following year.

From 1975 to 1977, 369 sets of negotiations resulted in only nine strikes (Downie, 1978). More recently, as the financial and unemployment picture has darkened, the impact, if not the number, of strikes has lessened.

Collective bargaining does not seem to have enhanced relations between teachers and boards, or clarified outstanding   issues. Although individual contracts have been negotiated, there is still much sparring for position between the two groups in general. Lam and Kong (1981) suggest five possible reasons for this state of affairs.

- Teachers and school boards differ over who should control such matters as teaching conditions, staffing procedures, staff development, instructional programs, educational finance, and professionalism.
- Trustees are concerned that most of the budget will calcify, leaving little for them to decide.
- Mutual distrust in collective bargaining frequently results in a deadlock.
- Teachers and trustees are establishing links between local bargaining units and central provincial organizations.
- There is a tendency to bring in outside expert help for negotiations.

It is not too early to study how collective bargaining affects the structure and substance of education.

9.3   Self-Licensing of Teachers

One aspect of professionalism is community sanction, including self-licensing. The qualifications and the reputation of the professionals are recognized by members of the community; they do not need official sanctioning by a legislative body.

Is the time right for the ministry of education to relinquish control over the issuing of licences to teachers? In Ontario, for example, the present movement towards this change is notable because it has, in principle, come from the minister herself. At the Fellows Awards Ceremony for the Ontario Institute for Studies in Education (OISE) on November 24, 1981, Dr. Bette Stephenson said she now saw the need to add the formal dimension of self-licensing. She had made substantially the same points at the annual meeting of the Canadian College of Teachers in July 1980.

Self-licensing is a logical step in a process that began with the Teaching Profession Act in 1944 and included the raising of entrance qualifications, the founding of OISE (to teach and research subjects necessary for professional status), and the active encouraging of professional development.

The minister's model for a "college of teachers" would include mandatory membership for all teachers in the public sector (that is, all present members of OTF). The "college" would set standards of admission and of certification, and would maintain all records. It would be separate from the teachers' federations. The governing body would include public representation as well as members of the profession.

The reaction of the OTF to the proposal is both positive and negative; positive to the concept, negative to the divorcing of its activities from the teachers' federations (Federation Update 1982).

Even a superficial perusal of the OTF position reveals many differences from the medical or legal models proposed by the minister. They differ on the questions of control and public participation in decision-making (Wing, 1982).

Wing appears to assume a unified body as proposed by the OTF. Most probably the minister insisted on public representation because teachers work in a publicly-funded school system.

One such model has been implemented. In Scotland, the General Teaching Council Act of 1965 certifies and registers teachers. Its powers and functions are similar to the General Medical Council.

Thirty of the council's forty-nine members are teachers elected by the profession. Fifteen others are appointed by various associations and institutions stated in the Act; four are nominated by the secretary of state for Scotland. All are expected to exercise independent judgement, not to act as delegates. The council is funded by a levy on members. It has no jurisdiction over salaries or working conditions; but it does issue licenses to teach after the probationary period has been completed.

The council may also discipline and "defrock" teachers found guilty of "infamous conduct in a professional respect." The council has advisory powers, for example, reporting on programs at colleges of education, and making recommendations concerning the supply of teachers and teachers' qualifications (Stabler 1979). It is plain that the Scottish model has influenced the proposal made by the minister; it is equally plain that the OTF believes this model does not go far enough. The federation would like control over licensing, discipline, and teacher education, preferably without public representation.

9.4   The Teacher in the School

9.41   Professional Growth

In-service training for the teacher comes under a number of titles— Orientation, Professional Development, Career Planning, Team Building—but should most often come under the title of Sharing. In-service training may be provided by a number of different agents or agencies: the principal, professional development committee, the superintendent, or the board. To be most effective, the teachers should be involved as much as possible.

Because there is so much to learn, the teachers should be willing to share with others and to learn from the experiences of others. The young teacher with new knowledge and the older, experienced teacher can complement each other. Together they can save many hours of work in preparing material for the classroom. In-service should start the moment the teacher enters that first classroom and should still be going on when the teacher retires. As a matter of fact, retired staff should be included in consultation and in project development.

The most effective in-service involves the teacher in the planning and delivery of the program. What does the teacher see as the real need? What would the teacher like to know about? Who can best deliver the information? Where and when can it best be obtained?

The answers to these questions can best be provided by the teacher, working in co-operation with a professional development committee of colleagues. The more involved the staff members are in the development of the program, the more likely they will be to participate willingly. Since teachers have different needs, the program must be flexible. Their experience and a knowledge of available resource persons will enable the committee members to put together a program on topics provided by the staff. Each staff member suggests the kind of program most needed.

An orientation day for staff should include information about the school, a tour of the building, delineation of supervisory duties, a social event, and an inspirational message from the principal to set the tone for the year.

The staff handbook is important for staff orientation and in-service. Besides the usual descriptions of what to do when organizing a field trip, the book should have a professional section with articles written by the staff on topics like "Qualities of Good Teaching" or "What We Look For When We Visit A Teacher's Classroom." "Qualities of Good Teaching" might focus on organization, communicating, human understanding, management, the teacher in the department, and the teacher in the school. "What We Look For When We Visit a Teacher's Classroom" might cover topics like the learning atmosphere, scholarship of the teacher, class preparation, lesson structure, objectives, continuity, motivation, standards, humour, judgement, involvement by the teacher and students, management, evaluation, rapport and discipline. This article should be rewritten from time to time as the standards of the school and its administration change.

A meeting must be held early in the year to explain how staff members are evaluated. When things go wrong, it is often found that no one really explained what was expected. If this is true for students, it is more so for staff.

Programs for the New Teacher. Teachers should be involved in programs for new teachers. They should ask the new staff members what they are interested in or what they feel they need. Often there is a teacher with considerable expertise in a particular area. That person should have the chance to help out. Teachers can also suggest sources from which new teachers can study other topics of interest at their own leisure. Sometimes the best programs can be visitation days in an experienced teacher's classroom. Such in-service can be arranged with minimum cost and disruption to the regular program.

Professional Development Days. Greater teacher power in bargaining has given the teachers more control over their own professional development day programs. However, they may have over-done it and lost public support. Perhaps the committees should invite the public on these days to take part. Professional development days are opportunities for all the activities mentioned above on a far grander scale, with better resources, and more money for better speakers on a wider range of topics.

The best professional development day programs involve staff with the same interests getting together to share ideas, methods and materials. Many teachers do this naturally and well. Unfortunately, some think that just because they spent the time developing the material, all other teachers should have to spend the same time. By sharing, everyone gains. Original work is like perfume: it must be shared to enjoy. One does not lose any fragrance by sharing it with others.

In-service for Up-grading. With declining enrolments, and new courses in the curriculum, it is vital that there be programs for the up-grading of staff. Frequently, one subject or program is affected more than others. If teachers in the affected fields can be retrained, they can keep their jobs. This obviously helps staff morale. Every school board should foster up-grading programs for staff. Someone in the board's development department ought to watch for programs with falling enrolment and new programs that need staff.

Too few schools have a continuing and wide-ranging professional development program. All schools could improve their programs.

Professional development programs should include something for everyone.

For the individual. Professional journals and materials should be made available. Staff who attend conferences should write brief reports for the rest of the staff. The principal should encourage the teachers to attend conferences and visit other schools. The teachers should be willing to pay at least part of the expenses. Teachers should visit industry and business establishments to learn more about the demands of the real world. Video-taped simulations are valuable.

Whole Staff professional development. The federations should conduct workshops at local meetings on such topics such as teacher "burn-out," drug education, and dealing with discipline. These should include a social time.

Beyond the school. Many schools should join together to share costs if a high-powered but high-priced speaker is wanted for a special reason.

9.42   Curriculum Development

Before 1965, the classroom teacher was not very involved in curriculum development. The teacher was expected to map out the lesson plans, but the courses of study came down from the ministry of education. The senior grades permitted little innovation because final examinations were administered province-wide and centrally marked under ministry control and direction.

At that time, the courses were put together by teams of experienced teachers, often with a university professor or two, working under the watchful eye of a ministry official. The examinations for senior grades — at first, grades 12 and 13 but later just grade 13 — were prepared by a university professor working with a committee of experienced teachers and set to cover the standard curriculum. These examinations were all written at the same time on the same day, all across the province, and they were marked by large teams of teachers hired for part of July at some central location.

A centrally controlled system has its advantages, but it must have the means for constant up-date and change. Many courses changed little over periods as long as twenty-five to fifty years. Teachers taught from the same little book of notes year after year. What innovation did take place usually happened at the elementary grade level where the teachers did not have to handle those provincial examinations.

Because of the standard curriculum and, especially, the standard examination, young teachers were seldom allowed to teach the senior grades. Only experienced pedagogues would do. The lucky teachers were those whose specialties, like chemistry, started in the senior grades.

After 1965, knowledge in many subjects was expanding so quickly that the curriculum had to become more flexible to keep up with a changing world. This was obvious in subjects like science. The change in education was brought about mainly by financial need. It was just too expensive to keep on administering the centrally controlled system as the post-war baby boom swept through the school system. Gathering and housing and paying those large teams of examination markers each July became impossible. So, the teachers were free to change the curriculum. Ministry guidelines were full of ideas on how to write and develop curriculum, but they gave little direction on what that curriculum should be.

Most teachers greeted these changes with joy. A few simply could not believe in what was happening; they tried to keep teaching from the same little black books of notes. The situation became chaotic. Where once there had been such rigid controls now there were almost none.

But teachers are, for the most part, fairly conservative and sensible. Although for a time things went off in all directions, some needed changes were at last taking place and the curriculum was catching up with the times. Secondary entrance examinations disappeared, and virtually every student could now go on to high school. This change triggered a much-needed revision in curriculum. To accommodate the many levels of ability among the students, high school teachers had to learn what elementary school teachers had known for a long time—one cannot teach the same things in the same way to all people.

At this point there was a tremendous push on the development of new courses as well as courses for different levels of student ability. The new Reorganized Program (colloquially called the Robarts Plan) provided at least two levels of study in most subjects. The development of the practical courses in the technical and business fields was now emphasized. Former collegiates became composite secondary schools. Various levels evolved now known as "advanced," "general," and "basic."

As could be expected, the teachers faced much pressure to develop these courses. But rarely were they taken from the classroom and paid to write new curricula. They did most of their writing in spare moments, often without much consultation. Level 4 (general) was often just level 5 (advanced) watered down. Inexperienced teachers were writing new courses because there were not enough experts to do the job. They made many mistakes. It is proof of the saying, "The kids learn in spite of the teachers," that schools came through that era as well as they did. Fortunately, many excellent curricula were written, tested, refined, and introduced into the classroom. Many of today's excellent courses came out of what was learned about writing curriculum for multi-level programs at that time.

Almost every subject added new courses. Enrolments expanded and expanded again. The secondary schools received a proliferation of new materials. The new credit diploma gave the students more freedom to choose courses. In 1969, students had to choose only areas of study, not compulsory courses. There were few prerequisites. Later, obligatory credits were re-introduced to ensure a rounded education. Art, business, physical education, science and technical education all blossomed out with a number of new courses. Even the old standard academic subjects, English, geography, history, and mathematics were expanded. There was some renaming of courses, Tyranny and Revolution instead of History, for example, and even renaming of whole departments, Home Economics became Family Studies, and Guidance went full cycle through Counselling to Student Services and back to Guidance. When the credit system was introduced in 1968-69, only with course calendars could one follow a student's program through the school.

Perhaps even more significant than all these changes were the changes in the late 1970's to introduce programs for students with special learning disabilities. At first, simple remedial programs in reading and mathematics were introduced. Later, there were more specialized programs to help students work in spite of certain disabilities. Young people ignored before the 1970's were now receiving special assistance from highly trained staff. Many are now taught to become as self-sufficient as possible.

Where does today's teacher fit in? It is a much different world from even a decade ago. Now new teachers, like the experienced teachers, must join a team at the school to keep the curriculum under constant revision and improvement. The new teachers can be most valuable here, for they are more apt to be up-to-date on methods and materials. On the other hand, the experienced teacher supplies the expertise to explain what children can be expected to absorb at any age. A modern school must blend youthful enthusiasm with experience to produce curricula that will truly help the student.

Two new factors, some would say problems, are notable. The ministry and most large school boards are tightening controls. At the same time, enrolments are declining. Now there are not enough students to take all the courses developed over the past twenty years. Teachers are competing for customers almost like businesses in the market place. This is a serious matter. The team leaders, — the principals and department heads — must make sure that all courses are necessary and not simply developed to attract customers to save teachers' jobs. Some courses may have to be cut back. Centralized controls are adding to this problem, for obligatory credits mean more compulsory courses and fewer options. Therefore, as some courses do not have enough students they will disappear. Teachers will lose their jobs. Strangely enough, the very program the government has been saying is necessary — technical education — may be one of the hardest hit. Most new obligatory credits tend to be in the academic fields.

The role of modern teachers is not an easy one. They are caught between a need to open students to many new studies and a tightening of controls that may narrow the options for the students.

9.43   Improvement of Instruction

Fads come and fads go and bandwagons pass by, but the best resource any student has in any classroom is still the teacher. The film projector, the television set, and now the computer, are all very valuable aids. But, they are only aids. They help the good teacher to be even better; they do not replace the teacher.

It is the teacher who motivates the students, who directs and encourages them, and who must care for them. Good curricula are necessary, television sets and computers are useful, support staff are helpful, but the teacher puts it all together.

Teaching is a very time consuming job. Sometimes the public sees only the school hours (9:00 a.m. to 4:00 p.m.) and the holidays, and assumes that teachers have it easy. But they are never there when the teachers are working to put the lesson plans together, preparing materials, directing the lay-assistant team, marking and evaluating students' work, and spending countless after-school hours helping exceptional students. When one adds the coaching and sponsoring of activities it is not hard to understand why teachers wear down. Not all students come to class eager to learn; not many learn completely on their own. The teacher is not just a director, but is also a real leader. Discipline is a serious problem. Another major factor is motivation—to make the student want to learn the subject and do a good job. If the student can be motivated, then discipline problems may disappear and true learning can begin. But the teacher must know the course and make the material meaningful for the students.

Motivation cannot be dealt with in detail here; it is different for each subject. However, some basic principles apply in most cases:

— The teacher must try to be interesting, to be lively without being a clown.

— The teacher must be enthusiastic. The student cannot be expected to get interested in something that does not even interest the expert.

— Ground rules are necessary. Students come to school to learn. They do not appreciate the disruptive person in the classroom.

— The teacher should use varied methods. It is good to have routines for standard management, with some variety in the presentations.

— The teacher serves as an example. Dress and speech must be appropriate. The teacher's actions must reflect professional standards.

— The teacher must work hard and be well-organized. The manner of dealing with the students should convey the message that the teachers have their best interests at heart.

— Each assignment must be checked, not necessarily collected and marked. It must be checked to make sure that it has been done. Students can put them on the corner of their desks. The teachers can check each as they circulate around the room during a seat-work part of the lesson.

— The students all have different abilities. The style of teaching should accommodate individual needs; for example, contract learning, small group assignments, tutor system. It is possible to assign tasks according to each student's capacity, and to evaluate accordingly.

— The teachers must get to know their students. But they must be friends, not buddies, take an interest without prying into their personal lives. Never quiz students about their homes or parents. If students trust the teacher, they will confide anything they think the teacher needs to know.

— Students should be introduced to different skills. The teacher should not assume they know what to do. The teacher should question them to check perceptions and allow students also to question. Do the students know how to do research, how to use the school's resources and the library, how to use the audio and visual aids? They should be encouraged to use these in making presentations to the class. The students must learn how to take notes, to study, and to write tests and examinations. They develop their memories by doing suitable "memory work." Teachers should encourage the discovery method and train the students to think before they speak.

— All teachers are communications teachers. All students, regardless of grade or ability level, can improve their communications skills. The lesson should include a variety of skills: writing, speaking, listening, and memory. These should be evaluated whenever possible.

The young teachers should learn to be generous with honest praise. They should respect honest efforts and look for improvement, for creativity, for ideas. They should avoid making comparisons among classmates, especially among family members. Sarcasm is an intellectual bully.

9.44   Working with Student Teachers

Is teaching really a profession? Although most would say that it is, the fact is that it does not pass one of the critical tests to be considered a profession. Traditional professions, like medicine and law, are self-governing. They control the admission to the profession, and they control the conduct of members once in the profession. Teaching is not truly self-governing.

Perhaps the closest that teachers come to having some control over those entering their trade is through the student teacher process. Students enrolled at the faculties of education spend short periods out in the schools as "apprentices" to practising teachers. These practising teachers are called "associate" teachers. They evaluate the work of the students and exercise some control over who is entering the profession. This is their only opportunity to govern the membership in the "union."

The periods the student teachers spend out in the schools are quite short, usually for two weeks at a time, and then possibly for only one week at a time with the same associate. The time may be very short but the influence is nevertheless very important.

Many people in the school can have an influence on the student teacher while the student is in the school.

The principal is perhaps the first person the students meet. Usually the principal greets the students and welcomes them to the school. Then, perhaps over a cup of morning coffee, the principal tells the students about that school and assures them they are to be considered staff in all respects and that the school will help them to do their best. Then, on a short tour of the school, the students will be introduced to the people running services available to the teachers. The students are then turned over to the associate teachers for further instruction.

The principal is very important in setting the standards for the associate teachers in the school. In the first place, the principal can encourage them to be associated with the faculty of education. This is an opportunity to participate in the screening and training of those who enter teaching. It provides the school with an opportunity to evaluate at least a few of the teachers available for job openings that year.

The department head or grade chairman is often one of the associates. This role may be passed along from one teacher to another if there are several experienced teachers in the school. In any case, the teacher in charge is the curriculum leader in that unit. The teachers in charge should allow the students to visit their own classes. They should share materials with the students and assist them with lesson planning. The teachers in charge should consult with the associate in that unit and participate in the evaluation of the student.

The associate teacher receives direction from the college or faculty of education about working with and evaluating students. The associate must not overburden the students; they must not replace the associate. The associate must be a model for the student. The associate should use a variety of methods with different grades and abilities. There should be frank and open discussion between the associate and the student.

The associate should assign fewer classes at the beginning of the year and at the beginning of the week. The students should be advised about what the class has been studying and what has worked well with them. They should know all the available materials. While the student teaches, the associate should stay in the room to be able to advise the student on changes in method or to compliment the student. Such advice should always seek to improve performance, not just to list the mistakes.

Evaluations of students tend to be too "nice." Associates should be fair but get the point across. Weak teachers must not be allowed into the profession. If in doubt, the associates should invite other teachers in for consultation. Total objectivity may be impossible, but they should be fair and helpful, and look for improvement the next day. If the student resists advice, this should be noted in the evaluation.

The younger staff can be very helpful. They can understand better what the student is going through; they were "in the same boat" recently. They can show the students how to overcome their nervousness. It may well be a good idea to assign a second or third year teacher as an advisor, to help the student find materials, secretarial and audio-visual services.

9.45 Judging Other Teachers

This dimension of the teacher's professional role arises seldom, if ever, in a formal way. Teachers are not required to submit reports about the performances of other teachers. No doubt principals sometimes seek advice, but teachers should be careful in offering it, and remember their professional duties. At times, it is difficult to refrain from commenting, especially when another teacher seems to be performing badly. It would be better to speak privately to the person to offer advice, rather than speak out of turn.

Sometimes, not often, judgements can affect relations with one's peers. This could happen in a team-teaching situation.

If they must make adverse comments, the teachers should fulfil the requirements of the regulation (Teaching Profession Act). They must provide a copy within three days to the teacher concerned. It is much more helpful to pass on compliments rather than criticisms.

9.46 The Teacher and Business Management

Some jobs performed by teachers are repeated every day for every class. Others are done only once a year. These the teacher cannot begin to understand until at least three full-year cycles have been completed. The management of time is very important to the teacher. Teachers often complain that they cannot get things done because of the paper work.

The average 40-70 minute lesson normally requires one to five hours of preparation time. If the lesson involves only researching of factual information, one hour may be enough. If the lesson requires support material—slides and projector, movie and projector, video tape and television set, records or tapes and player, wall charts, computer programs— then preparation may need many extra hours.

The teacher must also learn other factors in classroom management, the system for keeping attendance, for example. It is important to master the system early. The recording of attendance is a simple routine matter at the beginning of each class. If the system is kept simple, the information can be retrieved quickly. It is embarrassing to report that a student has been skipping class only to have the student prove that the teacher made the error. One class list can serve many purposes. The teacher takes the master list and rules adequate sized columns so this page can be photo-copied and used for monthly attendance, for marks, for assignments, for discipline records.

Marking is time-consuming. The teacher should keep the records on one photo-copied sheet. It should be clear how the system works because others may have to read the mark sheets. The sheet should show each test or evaluation, the total value of that evaluation, any weighting factor used, and indicate totals and what actually appears on the report card. Appeals of marks are possible, much more than a few years ago. During the summer, for example, the principal may be asked to check that evaluation and calculations were done properly. All schools store final examination papers for at least one year.

Another system that works well for any class enables the teacher to record individual data, marks, remarks, anecdotal reports, and to collate term marks. The same form serves as class list, a hockey list with practice times, a public speaking list with individual topics, a contract list with topics and groups, and an alphabetical list of parents' occupations and business numbers.

Regular size card stock are divided into 8 or 10 equal spaces, with names typed in alphabetical order on left side, the telephone number on the right. Photocopy 15 or 20 sets at the beginning of the year. These are three-hole punched and put in a binder. The class list will be easy to carry home for recording marks. If a teacher has more than one class to teach, lists can be colour coded. A set with a photo of each student would be particularly useful for multi-grades at the beginning of the year. One set could be kept near the telephone at home. For parents' night or for report cards, marks and a summary of comments alongside are close at hand. When the office asks for attendance record, a list of students who travel by bus or those who are coming on Saturday to set up the science fair, lists arrive immediately at the office.

The duties of the home room teacher are very time consuming: to keep attendance, read announcements, distribute and collect dozens of forms each year (insurance, lockers, timetables, photo appointments, guidance appointments, and assembly seating), explain school procedures (fire, attendance, assemblies, examination schedules), counsel students about problems and selection of programs for the next year, sell yearbooks, and collect student fees and money for school rings, pins, and jackets. How does one manage these tasks? The efficient teacher uses those same photocopied lists, keeps accurate records, and turns all collected money over to the office as soon as possible. Money should never be left in the classroom.

Administration of any class involves a wide variety of managerial skills. The average teacher performs many of the following tasks: arranging field trips for classes, giving first aid and filling out accident reports, selecting, and distributing textbooks, and then collecting them and assessing damages and collecting penalty fees. Other tasks include taking inventory, cleaning and repairing equipment, ordering, checking and storing equipment, and supervising events arranged by other teachers (sports, plays, music nights, assemblies, dances, etc.). There are also parents' nights or afternoons to arrange, parents to phone, report cards to fill out, graduations or commencements to attend, and committees to serve on. In any spare time the staff member may be called upon to coach or to sponsor special interest groups or even to attend a social event on the weekend.

This is why the term "administration" turns up frequently in teacher education programs. The following ideas may help the new teacher put things in order:

— *Learn to fight the paper war.* Try to handle paper only once. If a reply is needed, answer right on the memo. If a copy is to be filed, make a photo-copy. It is not necessary to keep copies of everything. Have paper organizers: desk trays, binders and files. Keep the system simple. Do not make filing systems too specific. Use a simple alphabetical file for most memoranda and letters. Review periodically and discard liberally.

— *Set priorities.* Sort obligations by the due date. Have three sections, a "do-in-a-day-or-two," a "do-this-week," and "do in the future." At the end of the day look ahead and move material forward. Plan for the next day. Use a desk tray or a binder with sections.

— *Use resources well.* Learn to delegate and to describe clearly what is wanted. If the instructions are clear, then the work will come back in useful form. If not, the work will have to be done again and again. In a classroom, never do what students can do; there are always some keen ones who want to help the teacher. Make use of the secretaries, lay assistants, technicians, the librarian, the vice-principal, and other staff members.

— *Plan.* Planning time almost always pays off. Lack of planning causes many mistakes; and correcting the mistakes costs more time than is needed to plan properly in the first place.

— *Work at the right time.* Certain tasks are best done at a certain time of day. During regular hours there are too many interruptions. Perhaps work could be done early in the morning or late in the day, in a quiet corner. It might be better to do tasks at school than at home. The necessary records and the equipment are at school.

— *Do not let the job get you down.* Everyone is under the same pressures. Look for the person who seems a bit better organized than the rest and try to learn from that person. Use other people's materials when they are willing to share and be prepared to share with others. Be on the lookout for better methods.

— *Say "No" once in a while.* Students can be demanding. Help them to be better organized. Set up appointments for student interviews at special office hours. But set aside personal time.

— *Get away from it all from time to time.* Everyone needs a few quiet moments, perhaps not every day, but at least a few times every week. Many teachers build into their personal schedule a few week-end retreats or personal renewal periods. There are many renewal centres open to all faiths, with qualified counsellors available on request.

9.5 Physical and Emotional Development

9.51 Work-Related Problems

Work-related problems are not new to teachers. But they have become more frequent, and now official notice is taken of them. Speaking at a workshop in Toronto in November 1981, George Meek, president of the Ontario Teachers' Federation, noted that as a counsellor of teachers, he was devoting much more time to work-related problems than he had been four or five years before. Teacher "burn-out" was the major problem, but there were others. These included assault (physical assault, property damage, verbal abuse and theft), general lack of respect in the community, marital discord, financial troubles, and morale problems caused by declining enrolment and the termination of contracts, whether actual or feared. The prospect of being moved from one school also caused stress in many teachers. Principals were no less affected; their response to both administrative and social problems touched the morale among school staffs.

Why is "burn-out" such a problem? In an address to a group of teachers in Toronto in February 1982, Stephen Truch noted three main characteristics of teachers in relation to stress:

— On the average, teachers die four years younger than the rest of the population.

— Next to air-traffic controllers and surgeons, teachers suffer the most stress among all other professionals.

— By a measurement called "burn-out," teachers break down faster than any other group of workers.

What is teacher "burn-out"? Truch (1980) defines it as "attitudinal, emotional and physical exhaustion to the point where a person cannot function properly in a certain capacity." This comes as the result of constant interpersonal contact with a number of people. Therefore, persons "who are unable to deal with this continued emotional stress begin to develop sets of symptoms which go contrary to the purpose they are trying to serve in the classroom" (Bancroft, 1982).

The public school system has been under attack for some time, both in ordinary community transactions and from the media. Educators are frequently asked hypothetical questions concerning schools; for example, "When is the curriculum going to be changed to include the basics again?" This is frustrating for the conscientious teacher.

It seems to the teachers that there are more and more restrictions on their professional autonomy, in the many provincial and municipal laws and the limits on salary increases. Another worrisome matter is assignment to other schools. Teachers understand that transfers caused by declining enrolments are necessary. The stress arises when they are not informed about changes, or they are not consulted.

Violence in schools is a greater problem in the United States, but there is evidence that violence is increasing in Canadian schools. The new Ontario Trespass to Property Act, 1980, which gives added powers to schools and police in the case of intruders, is one indication. Admittedly, there have been isolated cases of shootings, but schools do not yet need police guards by day. However, schools have hired them at evening functions (at which teachers are present to take responsibility) for some years.

Truch (1980) proposes a series of steps to combat burn-out. He refers to them by the acronym READ, where

R   is deep relaxation
E   is exercise
A   is attitude and awareness
D   is diet (although some refer to it as dialogue)

Truch writes that teachers must recognize "formal and informal ways of getting together to provide an effective stress management tool" (Bancroft, 1982). One of the most frustrating things about teaching is working in isolation.

9.52   Renewal, Refreshment, and Team Building
Teachers need to feel they are part of a team, where their own contribution is important. The wise principal or superintendent brings

the teachers from the different panels together, so that they appreciate what the others do.

Like most employees, teachers need to talk with their superiors from time to time. Who is the director of education? What is he or she like? Who are the trustees? How do they see our school? Are they supportive? Who are the consultants? What do they do anyway? Can they help? Why does the board have a psychology staff? Who are they? What do they do?

Teachers need to be introduced, gently, to new ideas and new fields and new interests. For example, many teachers have discovered new skills and hidden talents by learning about computers.

In-service for Advancement. Even in times of declining enrolment, schools need new administrators. There are always people interested in advancement, giving even more of themselves to young people, and having a greater influence on the development of educational programs. Such people need to be encouraged. Professional development or staff development or in-service can do it.

Too often teachers' federations emphasize the classroom and overlook the teachers who want practical experience in school administration. Teacher federations and school boards together should prevent rules from restricting the development of good people. For example, according to a Ministry rule, a teacher must have experience in three of the four divisions of education (primary, junior, intermediate, senior) in order to take the principal's course. Primary, junior, and intermediate are included in the kindergarten to grade 8 elementary school, but only intermediate and senior divisions are found in the secondary school. Obviously, the rule discriminates against secondary teachers.

The Costs of In-service. A good in-service would cost between $100 and $200 per teacher. Even then, it might not be enough to pay the salaries of supervisors of staff development. The cost may be high but it is important to have sound professional development and in-service.

Often, retired teachers are overlooked. Their experiences are valuable. Many would work as volunteers for expenses only, if asked.

9.6   The Teacher and the Law

9.61   Negligence

Teachers should know the laws governing education, and their obligations towards pupils.

Negligence is a form of tort. A tort is the term for wrong done by one person to another; a tort can be criminal (assault, battery) or civil (negligence, defamation). This discussion will be confined to civil torts, in particular to those of negligence and defamation.

The five elements of the tort of negligence are as follows (Thomas, 1976):

- A duty of care, recognized by law, existing between two persons.
- A standard of care, inherent in the duty, to which each person is expected to conform in relation to the other. When a person, who owes to another a duty under the law, fails to act according to the required standard of care, that person has been negligent.
- Injury or damage resulting to the plaintiff.
- A reasonably direct connection between the defendant's conduct and the resulting injury. This is usually termed the issue of "remoteness of damage" or "proximate cause."
- The absence of negligent conduct by the injured party. In other words, the court will ask itself whether or not the defendant was in some way negligent such that he contributed to or partly caused his own injury.

As far as teachers are concerned, "duty of care" is laid down in the Education Act. For example, section 235 requires them, among other things, to be responsible for order and discipline in the classroom, while on duty in the school and on the school ground. Section 236 charges a principal with the duties ("in addition to his duties as a teacher") to maintain order in the school and to keep attendance, among others. "Standard of care" is usually measured by what has come to be known as the "careful parent" test, or by its legal equivalent "*in loco parentis.*" In the exercise of their profession, teachers are considered to be "*in loco parentis.*" Therefore, they should exercise the care and control that might reasonably be expected of a careful parent. (See Teachers and the Law, 1974).

To be liable for negligence, actual injury or damage must have resulted to the defendant and a reasonably direct connection must be established between the actions of the plaintiff and the injury to the defendant. In addition, there must be an absence of negligence on the part of the defendant. This provision is sometimes interpreted in terms of contributory negligence; when awards are made, the original estimated damages may be reduced because of contributory negligence on the part of the defendant.

9.62 Vicarious Liability

Because they hire the teachers and principals, the boards are liable through what is called "vicarious liability"; that is, they are held responsible for the negligent acts of another person (the employee), even though they themselves may not be at fault in any way. This application follows the principle in common law of the "master and servant" relationship, by which the "master" in the relationship can be held liable for certain acts of the "servant," provided that what the "servant" was doing was normal work.

9.63 Occupiers' Liability

Boards may also be held liable through "occupiers' liability"—those who have control over the premises. In the case of schools, the controller or "occupier" is the board of education; hence, as a corporate legal entity, it may be sued. The Trespass to Property Act, 1980, re-defined the classes of entrants upon property and set out the standards of care. Generally speaking, there are "invitees," who are required to be on the premises (for example, a child is required to attend school), "licensees," who are using property but at their own wish (children playing in the school yard on Saturday), and "trespassers," who have no right to be on the property at all.

School boards must ensure that the premises are kept clean and in good order. Indeed, the Education Act requires them to keep the buildings in repair and to provide adequate accommodation. This requirement frequently extends to equipment, for example, gymnasium mats or laboratory equipment.

Another factor that determines liability is the principle of foreseeability. Accidents may be divided into classes: likely to happen, a possibility of occurring, and a slight possibility of occurring. Did the defendant in a case know the relative foreseeability? Were reasonable precautions taken to reduce or eliminate any likelihood of accident?

9.64 How Can Teachers Protect Themselves?

Accidents can occur anywhere, but generally speaking, some places are more dangerous: gymnasiums, industrial arts workshops, laboratories, school yards and field trips. (See *Accidents Will Happen: an Inquiry into the Legal Liability of Teachers and School Boards* and *The Legal Maze*. I. C. Barrett *et al.*, 1980.)

Teachers can protect themselves and their pupils if they follow the rules. Courts recognize that teachers cannot be everywhere at once. As long as a reasonable standard of care is being applied, teachers can feel secure. They must keep good discipline, whether they are on duty or not. The principals must see that teachers carry out these duties and understand the school's and the board's policies.

Teachers and principals should check that the board carries enough liability insurance. If it is insufficient, the federation could discuss this in collective bargaining negotiations. Judgements can run quite high, even above $600,000.

9.65   How Do Cases Evolve?

Usually there is little argument over the injury itself. The case revolves around the duty and standard of care. Was it a school situation? Did the teacher behave reasonably? Could such an injury or incident reasonably have been foreseen?

9.66   Assault Charges

Under Section 43 of the Criminal Code of Canada, teachers have some protection from charges of criminal assault:

> Every schoolteacher, parent or person standing in the place of a parent is justified in using force by way of correction towards a pupil or child, as the case may be, who is under his care, if the force does not exceed what is reasonable under the circumstances.

This section does not allow the teacher to hit every pupil in sight. Teachers must act like reasonable, conscientious parents.

9.67   Criminal Activities Unrelated to Teaching

Under certain circumstances, teachers can be penalized by suspension, termination of contract or even cancellation of their teaching certificates, for conviction of serious crimes not related to their teaching duties.

It is difficult to give a definitive list because standards and attitudes vary in different places. Drug offences, serious offences related to alcohol, and criminal offences all carry with them the risks outlined above. See section 235 of the Education Act.

9.68   The Issue of Defamation

The tort of defamation is concerned with a person's good reputation. According to the Oxford dictionary, defamation is the act of attacking someone's good name, or dishonoring a person by report. Defamation comes in two forms; libel, which is defamation by the written word or other permanent medium, and slander, by the spoken word or other transitory medium.

Should a person be sued for libel or slander and a judgement be given for the plaintiff, then damages may be awarded, as in cases of negligence. To establish defamation, publication is essential; that is, the statements objected to must have been communicated to a third party. Speaking one-to-one is not sufficient, but everyone with a part in publishing a libel or slander assumes responsibility for the consequences. In the case of libel, material that was thought to have been harmless when published can be held libellous, thus making the person who communicated it liable.

Qualified privilege does not extend to making statements ("publishing") about pupils, parents or colleagues when gossiping in the staffroom or wherever teachers congregate. And, though some statements are not exactly slanderous, such activities are certainly unprofessional and should be avoided; professional people do not discuss their clients or colleagues in a non-professional setting.

Qualified privilege extends to those statements that "are made in performance of a duty, in protection of an interest, are contained in privileged reports or are professional communications" (Williams 1976). The writing, sending and receiving of school reports is an example. Comments written on essays is another, although these would be published only if the recipient chose to do so. (Having a secretary make copies could be considered as publication, however.) Statements of evaluation of teachers made in the course of duty could be considered an example of qualified privilege. The regulation made under the Teaching Profession Act, Sec. 18(1)(b) requires, however, that "on making an adverse report on another member, [a member] shall furnish him with a written statement of the report at the earliest possible time and not later than three days after making the report."

What about the matter of references for former pupils? Williams (1976) counsels that these are in order because "inquiries made about a person with whom the inquirer is contemplating a business relationship will be qualifiedly privileged." Statements about others in the course of duty, whether they be reports, remarks, evaluations or references, must be factual, impersonal, and made in as professional a manner as possible. If criticism is necessary, it should be objective and without malice. For a full discussion of defamation and teachers, the reader should consult Pyra (1982), "Education and the Law of Defamation."

10 Classroom Management and School Discipline

10 Classroom Management and School Discipline

10.1 The Teacher as a Leader of Students

To change students' attitudes, one should first consider changing the teachers'. The teacher is second only to the parents and the home in influencing the students' behaviour and attitudes. They should set an example for their students to follow.

If the students are expected to be punctual, staff must be punctual. To discourage smoking among students, the teachers should stop smoking. To train students to be kind and respectful to others, the staff should treat students with humanity and consideration.

Teachers may be better educated, but in most respects they are just a cross-section of the people found in the community. But they have greater responsibility than the average person. They can influence the youth of the country. Therefore, they are expected to keep a higher standard of behaviour.

The spoken and written language of a teacher must be excellent. Teachers must not use profanity near their students. All teachers are language teachers; they should use good grammar and they should spell words and punctuate sentences correctly.

Teachers must be patient, willing to explain and to spend extra time helping others. If students see the teachers as a group ready to go that extra mile to help people, then the students will probably show the same kind of attitude. Perhaps not immediately, but slowly the students will show concern for their fellows.

All students should do the best they can. They are not all equal, but they can try. Here again, the teachers must set the example. It is unfair for the teachers to reprimand students for incomplete work, if the teachers themselves do not do their work. Students know whether a teacher is a hard worker.

Teachers should gauge their praise to the effort made by the student. If someone does an excellent job with little effort, then praise it but do not overdo it. If the student does a reasonable job through outstanding effort, then the praise should be lavish.

Students should respect their country, government and democracy. Freedom does not mean doing what you want whenever you want. It means responsibility and respect for others. Teachers can set the example. When the national anthem is played, they should stand firmly at attention.

Teachers can also prevent vandalism. Vandalism is not just breaking windows and kicking lockers and breaking plumbing fixtures in the washrooms. It includes the mess in the cafeteria, the garbage on the floor in the halls, the dirty equipment that clutters that counter at the side of the room. Are the teachers neat and tidy? Do they insist that students are neat and tidy? Teachers should discuss how to take care of things. By their actions, they show the students that they care for the building, that they care for the property of others.

It is difficult to correct improper attitudes. Often correcting someone else can cause arguments. But how can one set the example without occasionally risking embarrassment?

No matter what their age, students may not know what is expected of them. Often something goes wrong because the students were not told what was expected. It is better to direct them well in the first place than to reprimand them for not doing it the right way. Conduct in an assembly is a good example. At many school assemblies, especially those about sports, students cheer and even whistle and stamp their feet. Students believe that this is normal behaviour. Therefore, before taking them to a theatre or a Remembrance Day assembly, the teachers should tell the student right at the start that such conduct is not suitable and then explain what is appropriate. They will almost always follow such a lead as long as they know what is expected.

Fairness and mercy are necessary at all times, not just by staff towards students, but also vice versa. The student leaders, athletes and student governors must show respect for other students and for the staff. Teachers must instil the habit of thanking others for the efforts they make.

Teachers should not compare children with their older siblings taught in previous years. They must avoid remarks to the younger ones about the intelligence or behaviour of the older one. Such unfair comparison frequently hurts the younger student. All children should be judged on their own merits.

In the staff room, teachers must avoid gossip about their students. Frequently, a label about a student goes from teacher to teacher. The pupils sense this and react accordingly, by doing what seems to be expected of them. This is fine if they should overachieve. But if children are described as "dummies", they will probably live up to those expectations. This phenomenon has been described in many sources; perhaps the best explanation is in the book *Pygmalion in the Classroom* by Rosenthal and Jacobson (1968). Each pupil is a separate person who deserves to be treated on merit.

10.2 The Teacher as Leader in the Classroom

When thinking about entering the teaching profession young people seldom see the job in terms of leadership. But the first act of teaching is usually one of leadership—getting the attention and cooperation of pupils at the first meeting of the year.

Those with whom a teacher also has leader-follower relations include other teachers (in team-teaching situations) and para-professional assistants (library technicians, laboratory technicians, adult volunteers).

The legal relationship with pupils is, of course, somewhat different to those with teachers or ancillary personnel. The teachers are obliged to carry out certain duties that place them in an authoritarian position. They must keep order and discipline in the classroom, in the school, and on the school grounds. Pupils must obey such discipline as would be imposed by a kind, firm and judicious parent. How can a teacher combine keeping order with being a kind, firm and judicious leader? There must be rules in a classroom or school, as in any society. Rules change according to social change; few schools, if any, now insist that boys and girls enter the building through different doors. Yet, this was once the custom, even the rule. The best way to approach rule-making is to explain the reason. The teacher must not surrender the right to lead—in fact, may not legally do so—but an enlightened leader takes into account the views and feelings of the followers before making rules. Leadership requires the consistent, but judicious and humane application of rules, with appropriate penalties.

Dealing with adults is somewhat different. Leaders should not impose their decisions without consulting their followers. Followers are more eager to carry out those decisions in which they have played a constructive part.

Dealing with para-professional assistants is slightly different, for a teacher is more than nominally in charge. Again, however, the teacher should consult the subordinates because decisions made without their knowledge and participation are not so easily followed.

Authoritarian principals and teachers still abound (probably a higher proportion of the latter) but imperceptibly, modern leadership and management methods are infiltrating schools. This is true as new teachers arrive, as more and more groups seek to influence the everyday affairs of schools, and as participation in decision-making becomes more widely known and accepted.

10.3   Legal Requirements for Pupils
In the hierarchy of the school, the pupil is at the base. In many diagrams of lines of authority, the pupil is omitted completely. The instructions to pupils in the acts and regulations are quite brief; the Education Act has a few expressed indirectly. Regulation 262 has the most direct. Section 23 states that

(1) a pupil shall
   (a) be diligent in attempting to master such studies as are part of the program in which the pupil is enrolled;
   (b) exercise self-discipline;
   (c) accept such discipline as would be exercised by a kind, firm and judicious parent;
   (d) attend classes punctually and regularly;
   (e) be courteous to fellow pupils and obedient and courteous to teachers;
   (f) be clean in person and habits;
   (g) take such tests and examinations as are required by or under the Act or as may be directed by the Minister; and
   (h) show respect for school property.
(2) When a pupil returns to school after an absence, a parent of the pupil, or where the pupil is an adult, the pupil shall give the reason orally or in writing as the principal requires.
(3) A pupil may be excused by the principal from attendance at school temporarily at any time at written request of a parent of the pupil or the pupil where the pupil is an adult.
(4) Every pupil is responsible for his or her conduct to the principal of the school that the pupil attends,
   (a) on the school premises;
   (b) on out-of-school activities that are part of the school program; and
   (c) while travelling on a school bus that is owned by a board or school bus that is under contract to a board.

Sections 22 and 23 of the Education Act contain indirect references to the deportment of pupils. Principals may suspend pupils from school for certain deeds, including persistent truancy, persistent opposition to authority, habitual neglect of duty, wilful destruction of school property, the use of profane or improper language, and conduct injurious to the moral tone of the school or to the physical or mental well-being of others in the school. Boards may expel pupils whose conduct is so refractory that their continued presence in the school would harm other pupils.

These provisions collectively form the legal basis for the disciplinary standards in a school. In most schools, formal sanctions are applied only after other steps have been tried. The counselling or pastoral role of the teacher is obviously the first contact; most pupils respond at this level. Only those who exceed the reasonable bounds of the classroom face more stringent action. The same legal requirements form the basis for school rules that are given in writing to pupils, or else repeated to them in home-room periods or assemblies. The pupils should note them carefully. These rules make life easier. In some cases, such as failing to report an injury to the appropriate person, a pupil may face more serious, even legal, consequences. Rules are two-way streets, drawn up for the mutual comfort and well-being of the people in the institution. A students' council in a secondary school lets the students point to rules it considers inappropriate either in content or in application. In other circumstances, the situation is not so easily dealt with. That is why teachers and principals must know their pupils and act always like kind, firm and judicious parents.

The regulations certainly prescribe that pupils be diligent, but it should not be necessary to apply sanctions to remind them that the school is an institution both for learning and for socializing.

10.4 Legal Rights of Pupils

Pupils enjoy many of the legal rights of the ordinary citizen, but in some instances, these are somewhat curtailed.

It is possible that the new charter of rights in the constitution may change some long-standing customs; the school rules and regulations may be challenged in court if they abridge the ordinary rights and freedoms. The Education Act and Regulation 262 make it clear that enforcement of rules on discipline and personal appearance must be reasonable.

If challenging teachers and principals, the pupils must be aware of two principles:

- Presumption of validity: those in authority are presumed, at first glance, to exercise it properly.

- Test of reasonableness: pupils must submit to discipline that is reasonable.

Pupils also have the right to appeal to the Board a suspension by the principal. The pupils have the general right to lay criminal charges, for example, common assault.

Some boards have given certain rights to pupils. For example, in 1976 the North York Board of Education published a booklet entitled *Status of Students' Handbook - Students' Rights and Responsibilities.* One of the rights it conferred was the right to freedom of the press in the students' paper, as long as it did not endanger safety, was not libellous, or threatened to disrupt the educational process. In 1974, the Toronto Board of Education issued a similar booklet entitled *Students' Rights and Responsibilities.* This booklet referred to students' publications in the following terms: "Students must not publish or distribute material that is defamatory, contains personal attacks, includes obscenities or uses language which departs from the standards of the daily press."

A pupil assigned a locker has no real right of privacy. As long as they are acting in the best interests of the school (see "presumption of validity" above), teachers and especially principals may open lockers.

Pupils have a right to confidentiality of records. Teachers may use them only in the execution of their duties; no one else may see them except for appropriate reasons. With the proper permissions, a court may introduce them as evidence.

Giles (1978) wrote that:

Students' rights problems are usually solved within the school itself but sometimes present themselves as problems for central offices and school boards to cope with. Court cases, although not frequent in the past, probably will become more frequent in the future. For the classroom teacher, the legal hassle in the courts probably is not the worst side of an issue. As inconvenient, costly, time-consuming and embarrassing as a legal action may be, it is the side effects which usually are more harmful as far as the classroom situation is concerned. The emotional strain on both the students and the teachers mitigate [sic] against a classroom environment which is suitable for effective learning.

10.5   The Teacher as Evaluator

The legal basis for the evaluation of pupils is found in the Education Act, Section 236 (f) and (g):

It is the duty of a principal of a school

(f) to hold, subject to the approval of the appropriate supervisory officer, such examinations as he considers necessary for the promotion of pupils or for any other purpose and report as required by the board the progress of the pupil to his parent or guardian where the pupil is a minor and otherwise to the pupil;

(g) subject to revision by the appropriate supervisory officer, to promote such pupils as he considers proper and to issue to each such pupil a statement thereof.

Regulation 262, Sec. 23 (1) (g) states that one of the "requirements for pupils" is that they must "take such tests and examinations as are required."

When evaluating their work, teachers should first decide whether they are evaluating pupils or pupils' work. The two are quite distinct; evaluation defined here will be confined to performance and achievement.

First, the teacher must determine the objectives of the course. Then, what should be the criteria?

Besides being required under the Education Act, evaluation also improves learning and tells parents how the children are doing. Since criteria vary widely, caution must be used when reading another teacher's comments and evaluations.

Evaluation enables the students to see what went wrong, and the teachers to help them improve.

Evaluation can be carried out in many ways. These range from simple observation to full-scale examinations. Observation consists of noting data about children, their interactions with others, their use of equipment, the frequency with which they answer questions or volunteer answers. Tests come in many forms, including those constructed by teachers and those prepared externally for use as standardized measuring devices. Teachers should be quite sure of what it is they are trying to find out from the results of a test.

The examination, long the only method of evaluating in senior years and at universities, is still important. Indeed, in 1982, Ontario's Minister of Education announced that each secondary school pupil should write at least one examination each year. Teachers must teach examination construction and the writing of essays. Whenever possible, evaluation and marking schemes should be explained to pupils.

It is beyond the scope of this book to discuss details of the evaluative methods mentioned in this section. Readers should consult authoritative books on test construction.

10.6   The Teacher and Reporting to Parents

Parents are like the stockholders of a company — the school in this instance.

Formerly, report cards were entirely hand produced. Teachers wrote the marks in the squares on the report card and then wrote personal and helpful comments in a fairly large space provided for that purpose. The parent also got helpful hints on how the student could improve.

Then came the computer age. The machine prints the mark and the class average or median. It calculates averages so the teacher will not have to add and divide. It even prints comments from a list of acceptable remarks. Some teachers use this method but still want to write personal comments. Unfortunately, because the machine prints much smaller than a person writes, the little squares for the marks are quite small and the space for the comment is similarly narrow. Teachers became frustrated trying to fit even three or four words into these narrow spaces; more and more, they choose the computer comments from the master list. Now report cards have become so sterile as to be almost useless.

Those who complain about these reports are told they are old-fashioned. Can they not see that the advantages — accuracy and speed — far outweigh the disadvantages? If computers do make mistakes, it is argued that the errors were not at the school end; subjects and marks in the machine were simply not being printed properly on the report cards.

Is the speed really an advantage? The work has to be checked and often hand corrected before it is fit to be sent home. Is it really faster then? The teacher still has to enter the marks on a sheet. The machine can print stick-on labels with these marks to paste on the office record cards, but someone still has to stick the labels on and file the cards. The teachers and the secretaries have to hand correct all the reports and labels and record cards.

And computers take over a teacher's schedules. Certain things must be done at certain times to fit the computer schedule. For example, teachers cannot have the computer print-out back to help their promotion meetings because three days turn-around time is necessary. The end of June becomes chaotic. All schools in large school boards want reports at the same time. The computer bogs down. More errors creep in. Many a vice-principal has had to work part of July getting report cards straightened out.

Of course, computers are useful where the personal touch is not required. One solution is to use the computer to print the report card with names and subjects, and the teacher writes in the marks and comments. The computer-printed part of the report can be done weeks in advance. Any error can be corrected by a re-run.

It is important to keep in mind the following points when communicating with parents.

Parents generally want to be kept informed. But some will become annoyed at phone calls from the school because they never receive anything but bad news from the schools. They also deserve good news.

The parent or 18-year-old student has right of access to all school records. Records must be factual and accurate.

The school should publish its standards of attendance. This policy should include methods of reporting to parents, probably by phone. Calls may be made by the attendance secretary, home room teacher or subject teacher. If matters become more serious, then the vice-principal should call and point out the penalties. The calls to the parents should be accurate, business-like, and always showing real concern for the student. There should be some system to bring in extra help for the sick student, either at school or home.

Accurate attendance cards must be kept for each student. Photo-copies should be made available to the parent.

Evaluations of a student's progress should be sent to the parents. This should not be done only when results are poor. Some teachers have the parent sign the test paper before and after corrections are made by the student. It is important for the parent to see the student's work in its original form, with suitable comments from the teacher. Both the parent and the student should always be aware of the progress the student is making. There should be no surprises at the end of the term!

Some schools use an "early warning system" in the whole reporting and counselling and parent interview system. Around the fifth week of the term, after teachers have had time to get to know their students, the teachers explain, on a form, any problem they are having with a student which they cannot resolve. These are discussed in meetings. A team of counsellors and vice-principals look at those not yet resolved. The teacher is kept informed. Those problems left after all this are brought to meetings held after school and attended by all teachers of the students still on the lists. Here possible solutions are discussed. At least one person is assigned to help the student. Often this process includes a parents' night a week after these meetings. The method takes about three weeks.

Teachers should communicate with parents, by phone, by letter, or in person. They must stress solution as much as possible.

10.7   The Teacher and Attendance

The Education Act (Section 20) states that every child "shall attend an elementary or secondary school on every school day ... until he attains the age of sixteen years; and until the last school day in June in the year in which he attains the age of sixteen years."

From this, it appears that attendance at school is compulsory for all students under the age of 16. Other regulations, however, allow a special review for students who are a year or so under 16. These may leave school early if the parents or guardians request and if certain conditions of employment, education and supervision are met. Such cases are decided by local "Leaving School Early" committees, composed of representatives of the school board and the local community. These instances are few. Generally, the law expects the student to be in school through the age of 16 or until the end of June in the calendar year in which the student turns 16 (that is, the student need not return in September if the age of 16 will be reached before December 31st).

Many students do not really want to go to school. They find all kinds of ways to beat the system. As fast as school authorities find ways of checking, these students find new ways of evading the law.

Surprisingly, many parents willingly or by default help the student to play truant. But Regulation 262 places responsibility on the parent to report to the school on the student's absence.

At one time, schools demanded a medical note from the family doctor for prolonged absence or for missing examinations. Medical authorities, however, are reluctant to do so, for they are put at odds with their clients (the parent who pays the bills). Parents' groups object that the school asks for proof other than the word of the parent.

Some truants never take any record cards home for the parents to sign. They forge all records and notes with little chance of being caught. How can this be stopped? Schools do not have a limitless amount of secretarial or staff time to invest in phoning. Some parents are almost impossible to reach by phone during the working day. The student who plays the game carefully can get away with quite a lot. Using computers, many schools keep accurate daily accounts of class attendance; parents are telephoned even in the evening. Guidance and attendance personnel work closely together.

If the teacher cares and checks carefully, then skipping will be kept to a minimum. This is to the teacher's benefit. The teacher cannot teach those who are not there, and must spend many hours helping absent students catch up on missed work. If absence leads to school drop-out, then the enrolment of the school is affected and school budgets and staffs are reduced.

A few years ago in some schools, in California for example, attendance became optional. (At that time, even in Ontario, schools allowed students to do as they pleased when they had spare classes.) It was argued that what mattered was the mastery of the subject; some students could manage this without attending classes. (This makes one wonder about the quality of the course and the teaching.) Soon students by the hundreds were not going to class. The teachers did not object. The trouble makers stayed away and the climate for learning improved.

Almost every school has ways to bring the students back to class. One school, for example, requires every student out of class to carry a large square plastic tag with the number of the classroom from which the student was excused engraved on the tag. This tag must be carried in plain view and is so large that it cannot be put in pocket or purse. Another school co-operates with all the schools in the neighborhood and with the sheriff's department. On a day selected in secret by the schools, the sheriff's men pick up all school age children not in the care of their parents. They are taken to the lock-up and the schools send a person to identify and sort them. Then parents are called and required to come and get their children released. Of course, no police record is kept, but the parents are embarrassed and soon the students get the message.

Because the Act allows 18-year-olds to be treated as adults, they can sign for their own absence. The parents and schools have no say in the matter either. If the student decides to exercise this right under the law, all dealings with the school, as with any other agency, must be with that 18-year-old. Most schools still believe they work for the tax-paying parent and continue to report to the parent. Nevertheless, if the parent or the student requests that the school deal only with the student, then this must be done. In this case, the school should warn both the parent and the student that the parent will be left out of all decisions between school and student. The student takes full responsibility to obey school rules. With privilege comes responsibility.

The teachers must use the same methods in dealing with attendance as with discipline in general. They must make their expectations clear — an absence owes an explanation — but they must also be willing to listen. They should not be gullible. They must check up. Only in unusual circumstances should the students be excused from assignments; they are responsible for work missed during their absence.

The following are a few suggestions for the teacher.
- Know the school policy on attendance.
- Know the basic rules in the Act, and regulations.
- If uncertain, check with the school office.
- Be scrupulous in keeping records.

- Let the students see that you keep these records. Correct your records as you inquire about absences. Be up to date.
- Check the daily attendance sheet produced by the office to compare school attendance with your class attendance. Inquire about discrepancies. Be thorough.
- Check all students absent without authorization. Insist on explanations.
- Be sensitive. Do not embarrass the student. If you sense a delicate problem, ask the student to see you privately after class or after school.
- Check with the office or guidance counsellor for any extenuating circumstances relating to chronic absentees.
- Check with the home room teacher if there is a discrepancy between your record and that of the school.
- Look for attendance patterns:
  - X misses only a certain period (yours).
  - X misses certain days of the week (Mondays and Fridays are the most common).
  - X misses last period of the day. X misses period after lunch.
  - X usually misses tests.
- Always insist that students assume responsibility for course work missed and, in chronic cases, make up time as well.
- Telephone the parent. Express concern that the student is in danger of losing credit for the course. Have your records and the school records right there. They must be accurate. Use the same procedure on parent's night. Promise the parent that the student will get reasonable help to catch-up but that the student must come in after school and work hard.
- Talk to the person in charge of attendance. Outline what you have done and ask for advice and help. Inform the office of the situation and send the pupil to the office.

10.8 Discipline in the School

10.81 The Teacher's Role

For the new teacher, particularly at the secondary level, the advice and experience of a seasoned teacher is valuable. Teachers no doubt talk and worry about discipline too much. It is the worrisome side of teaching, the policing role that few really enjoy. Generally, people who want to teach are those who like young people. They want to work with them, to teach them—not to discipline them.

However, no one can teach students unless the students pay attention. Lack of discipline means lack of attention; a teacher cannot teach those who lack discipline. Thus discipline must be imposed by the teacher.

The experienced teacher knows that getting off to a good start at the beginning of the year or semester is crucial. The strong teacher has little problem setting the proper tone. Certain routines become a part of that teacher's nature. But even experienced teachers, when they move from one school to another, often find that they have to work a little harder at establishing tone that first year in the new school. Their reputation from the previous school does not travel with them. One such teacher came into the vice-principal's office to complain — "These kids are trying those new-teacher tricks on me."

What works for one teacher does not always work for another. Good discipline does not mean a loud voice or a heavy hand or large stature. Some of the best disciplinarians are soft spoken and petite; the worst, loud-mouthed and large. The students soon get to know those who mean business; they also recognize a bluff.

There are many ideas of discipline. Not all are wise, like the following misguided ones:

   — "If I am nice to them they will be nice to me."
   — "As long as you keep your troubles inside your own classroom you will be all right."
   — "Oh, it's just a big game. They win some and I win some. As long as I win more than they do, then I am a success."

Teaching is not a game. It is a profession. If teachers are going to be reasonably successful, they should follow good, sound practices. Here are some of the things young teachers must train themselves to do.

Be organized. Know the school rules. Do not threaten sanctions that are not in the rules and for which there will be no administrative support. The students know the rules. Have lesson plans well prepared. Know exactly how to start, where the lesson is heading, how it is to end. It is not a bad thing to digress from a lesson plan as long as you know you make the digression a short loop that comes back to the main stream. Have all support materials ready and available (seating plans, for example). Have paper supplies, chalk and audio-visual materials right at hand. Do not leave the class unattended while you go looking for them. Check out all equipment in advance. Be sure that demonstrations will work.

Set clear and reasonable rules. Every classroom has some simple "do's" and "don't's." Laboratories and shops will have some "don't touch" items.

Teachers should direct the students to come into the room in an orderly fashion, go right to their seats and get their books and pens ready for action. In a calm and composed manner, state your rules just as though they were unique. Most disruptions can be traced back to unclear statements of expectations.

Teach at the right level. This is the hardest of all things to master. If you make things too easy, students will be bored and look for other things to do. If you make things too hard, they will soon give up and start looking for ways to disrupt. If you go too fast, they will look for ways to slow you down; if you go too slowly, they will have time for mischief. If things are not going well, look for clues that you are beyond them or below them, going too fast or too slowly. Make small adjustments and look for the effect on the class. Discuss your materials and methods with your department head or senior colleague, and ask for advice.

Keep cool. Everyone makes mistakes. If you are well-organized, you will not make as many errors. Do not blame mistakes on others. Accept them as part of doing a difficult and complex job, and get on with it. If it can be corrected right away, do so. If it cannot be corrected immediately, put it to one side and promise to come back to it tomorrow. Be business-like. Do not ignore the problem.

Problems include the following:
- There may be pushing and shoving and horse-play as students enter the room. They may be too loud and talk through the lesson. They may drop things. They may be late.
- They may fail to do assigned homework. They may obviously be ill prepared for the work of the lesson (perhaps not knowing what was taught just yesterday). They may do things in a sloppy fashion.
- They may want to argue or be rude. They may even shout and swear at you.
- They may fight among themselves, starting with name calling and progressing to physical violence. They may throw things at each other.
- In very rare cases, they may become violent toward you, starting with swearing and then proceeding to physical violence.

Obviously, there is a great deal of difference in the descriptions listed above. It is important to remain as cool as possible.

In cases of horseplay, pushing, shoving or loud talk, it is important to note carefully who was responsible. The teacher must deal with the situation immediately, but also bring it to the attention of the class: "John, stop that shoving!" "Maria, be more quiet!" "Susan, you are late for class. What is your reason for being late?"

Then, in front of the class, especially if others were involved but to a lesser degree — "John, as you were coming in today you were doing a lot of shoving and general horse-play. That is not acceptable in my classroom! I expect you to know better! I will watch for improvement. If you show you cannot improve on your own then I will have you in after school for some practice in how to do things properly." "Susan, if another teacher keeps you late after class I expect you to bring a note from that teacher. Otherwise, I must assume that you are taking advantage of my good nature. You are making me take valuable time away from the class. We might be in danger of not getting the lesson done on time and might have to do extra work after school."

In all of these cases, there is the gentle mention of the possibility of after school work. Repeated threats become meaningless and futile. If the problem occurs again, the student must stay in after school. The student must catch up any work missed. The teacher should not display anger, and should remind the student of what was wrong and that a warning had been given.

Homework must be checked. While the students are doing their seat work, they open their books and the teacher takes a quick walk around. The students are warned, quietly but so all can hear, that all assigned work must be done or the student must come in after school. If a number did not do it, the teacher makes a general announcement to the class. This applies to all work not done: homework, project, preparation for class, and study for tests.

Teachers should not argue with the students in front of the class. Simply state the point as calmly as possible. Tell the student that any discussion will have to be held after school and make a timed appointment. If the students want to continue to disrupt the class, tell them you will have to insist that they report to the office. If the students persist, they must report to the office at once. Go to the P.A. and tell the office that this student (by name) is being sent to the office. After the class see the student briefly and re-confirm the appointment for after school. Then go back to class.

All cases of insolence, swearing and rudeness must be dealt with after school. There is no "one free warning." As in all other cases, make it clear what was wrong and what you expect in the future. Make accurate records including the exact words that were spoken.

In all cases of swearing at the teacher and in all cases of physical violence toward other persons, the case must be brought to the attention of the office. All schools will have procedures for doing this. Violence by word or action must not be tolerated.

In the very rare case of violence toward the teacher, you must get help immediately. Use the P.A. or get a nearby teacher. Do not try to deal with the situation by yourself. You may be able to handle the situation but if you end up in court, you will be glad of witnesses.

Have a busy classroom. Students busy at work cause few discipline problems.

10.82 The Principal's Role

The law says the principal is responsible for the discipline in the school. In setting up the rules for the school, it is good to involve both staff and students. The principal should always sit in on these discussions to prevent the committee from deciding on something that cannot be supported. It is easier to do a little steering of the committee as it goes along, than to have to veto their final report. The principal gives leadership and advice, and tries to link the consequences to the act.

All parties should be told how to handle certain situations. They must follow simple and clear procedures and keep good records. Vice-principals are educators and must be allowed to exercise their own judgement. Suspension, one of the toughest discipline measures, must not be overused or abused. The principal should tell the parents what the duties of the student are; parents also have a responsibility to help the school.

Discipline in a school is a team effort. If employees are confused, then discipline will be poor because staff morale will be low.

10.83 Counselling

The traditional view of the teacher encompassed many roles, one enshrined in legal terms as the kind, firm and judicious parent, and in the concept of *in loco parentis*. The teacher was a surrogate parent. In former times, this responsibility was accepted gladly and with comparative ease.

Today, the school systems include counsellors specializing in helping pupils make choices. Computers make it even easier to get information. The counsellor also deals with the common emotional problems of children. Many pupils, in secondary schools particularly, consult counsellors to help solve their troubles, both academic and social. Younger children turn to their teachers for help.

Where does all this leave the teacher, in particular the home-room teacher? A child or young person still needs a sympathetic, interested person to turn to; teachers may be expected to fulfil this role. If a problem is too difficult to handle, they should call in a specialist. Afterwards, whatever the outcome, they should talk to the students to see if there is anything more they can do.

The teachers pursue the pastoral side of their jobs by taking an interest in all pupils, especially those in their home-rooms. A few minutes to talk here, to ask questions there, to compliment someone else, to listen to concerns all go a long way to achieve the social goals of the school.

10.9 The Teacher as Coach or Sponsor

A good teacher likes children and shows this by becoming involved with them beyond the walls of the classroom. They find some common interest to share with the students. One should not become a coach or a sponsor to win a popularity contest. And those students taking part in the activity need not be those of the teacher's classes.

"Extra-curricular" activities are so called because they take place after regular school hours. They help teachers do their work in the classroom. As has been noted, the teachers must get the attention of the students before they can teach. One important way is to appear as an interesting and worthwhile person. Then the student will have faith that what is taught is also worthwhile.

Extra-curricular activities that attract most attention are sports. By their very nature, they are competitive. The less-competitive teachers and students join groups in drama and music and art and clubs for the mind (chess, computer, mathematics contests), for service (Junior Red Cross), and to practise citizenship. All need leaders and followers.

The coach or sponsor can be a good example to the students. In sports, for example, they learn the obvious sportsmanship and fair play.

The coaches and sponsors can also help the failing students. Often the extra-curricular activities give students the incentive to stay in school, especially if they are failing or are bored. Thousands of students have stayed to graduate because of a love for a sport or activity and the relationship developed with the coach or sponsor.

Extra-curricular activities can be divided broadly into two categories: sports and citizenship. But they do overlap.

Sports must include activities at various levels. Of course, some must be segregated, restricted to boys or to girls, or to certain ages, but some can be mixed. The "star" can develop skills beyond the average in inter-school competition, and the average athlete can play just for fun. There should be team sports and individual sports. Above all they must develop good habits for later in life. For many people, physical well-being depends on getting some exercise, probably by playing a sport.

Citizenship activities take many forms. Some are service-oriented: student government, prefects, library club, yearbook. Some have a message: Christian fellowship, campus life. Yet others are subject-oriented: archaeological club, art and poster club, science club, photography club, band and choir, debating club, drama.

Many students join more than one group. There lies a problem. All these activities demand considerable time. The sponsors must work together to set practice schedules so that students can take part in many activities.

Today, there are more special "enrichment" programs for the gifted students; many take place after class. Often these students feel left out in the classroom.

It might be said that the whole extra-curricular program is really an enrichment program for everyone, not just for the gifted.

Those working with the students after school are sure that these students cause less trouble than those who leave at the closing bell. Fewer hang around the plazas and street corners to get into mischief or just waste their time. It is a great contribution that teachers make to society through coaching and sponsoring after school activities. Unfortunately, parents and even the school board fail to appreciate the countless hours of voluntary work done by teachers. The students themselves often do not recognize what the teachers are doing for them. If the team wins a championship, they praise the coach; but they say little about the coach who works just as hard and long but loses the game. And the sponsor of a service activity or subject club is ignored even more. The rewards come from the smile of a student in the hall and the odd "thank you" from a student after the season is over. But the real benefits are in the classroom. The teachers know they have given something of themselves and have inspired young persons toward a better attitude.

11 Staff Hiring, Evaluating, and Firing

11 Staff Hiring, Evaluating and Firing

11.1 The Principal and Staffing

A principal's most important task is hiring staff. With the right staff, there will be good teaching. With perfect teachers, the principal would have to perform only administrative roles. Hiring staff involves many factors: for example, enrolment projections, and negotiations with the superintendent, deployment of staff, and interviewing applicants.

11.11 Staffing a School

Before deciding what staff is needed for the following year, the principal informs the students and parents about the courses to be offered and asks them to make selections. In the early fall, the principal discusses with senior teachers* the courses to be offered. The principal keeps these suggestions in perspective and does not let one area overshadow another. What is on today's curriculum that will not be needed in tomorrow's world? What new courses should be developed to prepare the student for the future? In the case of secondary schools, course descriptions are published in calendars, with general instructions about obligatory credits and what totals are necessary to graduate. The student and parent fill out an option sheet to register the courses they want. The calendar is prepared in the fall so that the course selections can be made in January, and schools can be ready for staffing decisions in March.

A computer tallies the data from the option sheet. Using these calculations the principal can determine the courses, class sizes and necessary staff.

---

* "Senior teachers" is used in this chapter to avoid the terminology "teachers in charge of organizational units" found in Regulation 262.

In January and early February the principals of elementary and secondary schools try to predict how many students will register the following year. Grade by grade, the principal looks at the current enrolment and estimates what proportion will move on into the next grade. In the lower grades, students are not yet of school leaving age; they can be counted on to stay. In the upper grades, however, some leave, depending on the job market and many other factors.

Finally, the principal submits this enrolment projection to the appropriate superintendent who, in turn, transmits it to the superintendent of planning. Here there may be some negotiations until a final figure is agreed on. The staff to be assigned to the school is then calculated according to the board's formula.

Often, the number of staff to be hired is lower than the school would like to have. There must be cutbacks and classes will be larger than were originally planned. Perhaps fewer counsellors, librarians or specialized teachers will be assigned. The school must operate with the staff assigned.

Adding staff brings new ideas, and the chance to see new teachers develop. Losing staff means deciding who must go and trying to help them to get placed in other schools. If possible, the principal tries to fit people into other departments or divisions. Usually, this process is completed by late February.

Today, many federation contracts specify that cuts must be made according to system seniority but taking competence into account.

Over-riding all these considerations is possible surplus of staff within the whole school system. If the system needs fewer than the total number employed, then certain employees of lowest system seniority will be laid off. The principal cannot count these people as part of the school's staff. The staff redundant to the system must wait for vacancies in the total staff needed by the system.

Voluntary transfer to other schools is open not just to those declared surplus in a school but to all staff members. This goes on for a month or so, until April.

Now comes the time for "administrative transfer." The surplus people must be fitted into the available slots, if that is at all possible. A superintendent and the principals together consider each surplus person one at a time, usually by seniority. If there are no jobs for which the staff members are qualified, they may be eventually declared redundant. Many collective agreements keep a few such people on staff in the hope of placing them later.

Only then can there be external advertising. Faculty of education graduates now apply, are interviewed, and hired.

Those still on the redundant lists are not discarded. Before an advertisement can be placed, the hiring committee checks to see that there are no suitable people on this list of redundant staff. The system is still trying to place them.

It is surprising how many of these people eventually are placed. Peel Region in Ontario, for example, has had as many as 100 on the redundant list; all were placed by the following fall. Many jobs open up during the summer. And teachers leave for short terms because of illnesses, professional development, and maternity leaves. There are jobs advertised in the newspaper almost every day of the year.

11.2   The Principal and the Evaluation of Teachers

The principal is the boss, the one who writes those life-and-death reports about staff. In a large school, staff evaluation takes up much of the principal's time, especially if it is done as some federations and boards recommend. Some areas of the evaluation are covered by law, regulations, policies, or contracts. Because a few evaluations may recommend termination of contract, the procedure must be legally watertight, and the staff member must be treated humanely. This usually means several evaluations with recommendations for improvement, assistance, and time for improvements.

One problem in any evaluation—it may well be questioned in a hearing—is the matter of the principal's competence in doing the evaluation. No principal can be an expert in every subject; how then can one evaluate the teacher fairly? In response, many principals are assisted by a senior teacher. Unfortunately, the federations have recently added clauses to their policies that teachers should not be making written reports on other teachers. Many people urging such policies think they are working in the best interests of teachers but is this really the effect? Is it not better to be evaluated by someone who knows the subject than to be evaluated by one who never taught that material and knows little about the special methods and difficulties involved? Surely the term "teacher in charge of an organizational unit" implies some degree of supervision of staff, and hence evaluation of staff. Surely, no one wants to return to the days when the teacher-in-charge spoke to the principal about the staff member, but nothing was in writing and so the staff member knew nothing about this. The senior teacher must be involved; in fairness to the teacher, everything said must be in writing with a copy to the teacher.

The Act states that teachers cannot be on probation for more than two years if they have fewer than three years of experience when signing a contract. They cannot be given more than one year of probation if they have three or more years of experience.

A problem arises with the one-year probation. Staffing decisions for the following year are made by the beginning of March each year. This means final staffing evaluations in a teacher's probationary year must be completed by February. Thus, a teacher who starts with a school in September has only about six months (until February) to prove competence. If, in the mid-fall, the principal is not satisfied with the teaching, there is very little time to go through the stages of defining the problem, giving assistance and time for improvement, visiting again, perhaps suggesting further work and re-visiting. It is a very tight schedule. Trying to be fair to the teacher, the decision-makers have actually made it almost impossible for the principal to give the teacher enough time to meet the standard.

Some boards and federations have worked out a plan for evaluation involving some or all of the following steps:

— A pre-visit session where the principal and teacher discuss the lesson to be visited and the objectives of the lesson plan
— A visit to the classroom for observation of this lesson
— A post-visit discussion of the lesson, evaluating whether objectives were reached
— Perhaps further rounds of these three steps, especially if any problems were observed on the first visit
— A discussion with the teacher before writing the official report
— The writing of the report
— A post-writing discussion with the teacher, with possible changes or revisions to the report
— A re-writing of the report, if necessary

Depending on the length of the classroom visits and the discussions sessions, it can take several hours to complete the cycle and get to a final report. If probationary staff are to be evaluated twice each year and a part of the experienced staff are to be evaluated once each year (most boards expect a report on a staff member at least once every three years), then the evaluation of staff can take hundreds of hours of the principal's time. This is impossible. Here is a more sensible approach to staff evaluation, using resources common to most schools:

In September, the teacher gets used to the procedure of the school. The principal does not visit the classroom unless requested to do so by the teacher or by the teacher in charge. The latter does visit and gives the teacher all possible help and advice about objectives, methods, and classroom management. He or she then writes an informal report on the classroom visit and gives a copy only to the teacher.

Few teachers like to be warned of the principal's visits, but the teachers have that privilege. Many teachers become nervous and do not do their best if they are warned; occasionally something happens to the principal's schedule so that the visit does not take place.

The principal should hold an after-school meeting to outline procedures with all staff due for reports that year.

In October and November, the teacher in charge continues as above but now the principal (and perhaps vice-principal) starts a regular round of visits. Whoever visits the teacher for evaluation should produce a visitation report, with a copy for the teacher. If serious problems are observed, there should be an immediate meeting with the teacher and perhaps the teacher in charge. Here the necessary improvements would be outlined in detail and the assistance of the teacher in charge clearly defined. A specific time for future visits might then be arranged. The teacher would be given a minimum of a few weeks to make the improvements, which might carry on well into December.

Assuming all is going reasonably well, the teacher in charge produces a formal evaluation report, discusses it with the teacher and, with the teacher's approval, forwards a copy to the principal. The principal then meets with the teacher to discuss the evaluation submitted by the teacher in charge and the observations by the principal during classroom visits.

The teacher suggests additions or changes in the formal report written by the principal. This is very important—the staff member's future is affected by it. The staff member should be able to suggest items for the report. The principal then writes the report and signs it. The teacher reads the report, signs and attaches a private comment to the report, if so desired.

If the teacher is on probation, this cycle is repeated in January and February; a final report with contract recommendation is written no later than March. If the report is about an experienced teacher, this cycle might well be done later in the year; the final report is completed no later than May.

All reports about probationary staff include recommendations for improvement; these might be in the form of compliments if the teacher is already doing as well or better than one could expect. The reports about experienced staff are usually longer, with comments about the progress of the teacher since the last report was written.

These reports do not have enough compliments. At least 90 per cent of the teachers deserve them.

The evaluation of heads or chairmen should be similar to that of the teachers, insofar as the classroom teaching is concerned. Here it is even more important to involve the vice-principal because the senior teacher does not take part. There should also be an evaluation of the teacher in charge. This evaluation must involve discussion about the program in the organizational unit, the use of staff and resources, and the organization of the unit. There should also be a section on how the teacher in charge shapes school policies.

11.3 The Principal and Staff Dismissal

Sometimes the principal must dismiss a teacher to protect the interests of the students.

There are so many ways of teaching that it is often very difficult to define why a certain teacher is not effective. Much of what is said may be merely personal opinion; rarely do any two principals agree on what they are looking for in a teacher. Few employees have the latitude a teacher has. It is so difficult to prove that a teacher is ineffective and is using the wrong methods, that many believe, with some justification, firing a teacher is impossible.

If the teacher is obviously corrupt and immoral, there may be no problem in firing the teacher.

If it can be proved the teacher is cruel to the pupils, there may be little problem in firing. Many people, students and staff, may be willing to give evidence.

It is almost impossible to dismiss someone who is "nice" but a poor teacher, unable to keep good discipline or to teach the curriculum or to evaluate the students. This is especially true if the teacher is popular with students and staff. Sometimes the senior students will be upset about poorly taught classes, but the junior students will rarely complain. Gathering evidence will involve many visits to the classroom and all this may appear to be merely a difference of opinion.

It is next to impossible to dismiss the teacher who is effective in the classroom but is insubordinate to superiors, perhaps refuses to attend meetings or to take part in after-school activities.

Supervisory officers frequently tell principals that it is their duty to get rid of ineffective teachers. These same administrators, however, are often so afraid of legal action that they suggest principals consult with the superintendent before writing any unfavourable reports about them.

The teachers' federations also insist that principals have the authority to dismiss ineffective teachers. They even stress that it is the principal's duty to do so. However, when disputes arise, the federations seem to side with the teachers. Perhaps there should be a neutral forum to decide what is best for the students.

Teaching is a difficult job, and the teacher education programs are too short and there is not much opportunity to learn on the job. An apprenticeship and a longer probationary period might be in order. An apprenticeship is better for it implies that there is close supervision. On probation, the teacher gets little more supervision than a teacher on a permanent contract.

In the end, it is up to the principal to judge how well the teacher is doing. Therefore, the teacher must have every chance to meet the standard the principal demands. The teacher must also have the chance to try again in a different school with a different principal before being finally dismissed.

If one lesson is unsatisfactory, the teacher deserves a clear explanation of what was wrong (by the standards of that school and principal) and what must be improved. This should be written out. What this principal wants may be the opposite of what the teacher learned at the faculty of education and from associate teachers during practice teaching. The principal must explain carefully what is wanted.

The teacher is entitled to a reasonable period to improve. Changes cannot be made overnight; a month is a reasonable time. During this time, the teacher in charge should again help the teacher as much as possible.

If, after a couple of months of advice and chances for improvement, there are still not the necessary changes, then the teacher should expect action. As much as possible of this should be in writing. By now, the first official report has been written. This should draw in the superintendent and possibly the federation.

The superintendent reviews the documentation with both the principal and the teacher. Has the principal been thorough and fair enough? Does the teacher understand clearly what is expected? The superintendent then arranges a visit to a class or two and writes a detailed report to the teacher and principal about these observations. The superintendent must understand clearly why the principal is not satisfied.

The principal may consult the superintendent before dealing with the federation. This is not absolutely necessary, however, since the principal can consult the federation without the approval of the superintendent. Politically, it is prudent to keep the superintendent informed. It is also wise for the principal and the teacher to ask for joint consultation with the federation. Perhaps some of the principal's resentment towards the federations in such cases occurs because the principal rarely consults the federation. As it is usually the teacher who turns to the federation, the federation acts as though the teacher is the client. A joint consultation allows the federation to act as a mediator rather than as a representative of one party against the other.

If all the steps outlined above have taken place and it is now well into winter, with little or no improvement, then the principal must recommend termination of contract. What happens now is up to the teacher.

The teacher may resign. The teacher may ask for another chance in another school. Or, the teacher may request a hearing with higher levels of superintendents or the federation. As last resort, the teacher may wish a board of reference. This is a serious step, quite costly in legal fees. This is more often taken by experienced teachers than by young, new teachers — it can become quite embarrassing if all the facts are presented in an open, court-like situation.

11.4 The Principal and Staff Promotion

Promotion is a mixed blessing, good for the person moving up but bad for the school losing a valuable worker. Nevertheless, it is important for staff morale. Even those who have not yet applied for a promotion are encouraged when their colleagues get new chances in higher places.

Promotions take place in different ways. The principal may identify and encourage certain staff members. The superintendent may identify staff the principal overlooked. And, certain employees the principal would never have considered for promotion may apply; sometimes, they get the jobs instead of candidates the principal was supporting.

How can a principal help promotions?

- The principal should learn the career plans of as many employees as possible. During staff evaluation, there should be a time to talk to them about their goals. Perhaps the principal could keep lists of those interested in promotion. The principal can notify the right people about any courses or openings.
- The principal should inform the staff about courses and qualifications necessary for promotion. They must also be told times for application deadlines and procedures for promotion.
- The principal should give teachers opportunities to develop skills and show responsibility by joining committees, taking on chairmanships, and working in the office on attendance, examination schedules, timetables, or duty rosters.
- The principal should offer help and advice. Few employees have had much experience with the kinds of interviews they need for promotion. They make the mistake of thinking they will be asked about the job they are now doing; in fact, they will likely be asked

more about the job they are applying for. They should be encouraged to investigate the position, to go to the interview as well prepared as possible. Simulated interviews can improve their interview techniques.
— The principal should discuss with the teachers in an open and honest way what they see as their greatest strengths and weaknesses. The staff members should see themselves in a realistic light. The principal can also tell them whether they seem ready.
— The principal should give an honest assessment when asked by a prospective employer. It should reflect comments already communicated to the staff member in person.
— The principal should sit down with an unsuccessful applicant and discuss the following: what was actually heard at the assessment; what can be done to improve; how the necessary experience can be acquired; and when it would be appropriate to re-apply.
— The principal must keep accurate records about all teachers, especially those looking for advancement. This helps to make clear statements with little hesitation. A principal who has faith in the staff member should say so with authority supported by reasons.
— The principal should encourage the best teachers to move up the ladder. The school may not want to lose them, but the system needs good people.

11.5 Declining Enrolment and Redundancy

Until recently, teaching was considered one of the most secure jobs. Those days are gone. Even the teacher on permanent contract, the one who used to have absolute tenure, is not safe if enrolment in that teacher's subject declines.

Despite declining job opportunities, the faculties of education are reluctant to limit enrolment in teacher education courses. (Some restrictions have recently been imposed.) They say they provide an education, just like any other faculty of the university; they have never promised jobs at the end. Competition for jobs is very keen. Many qualified teachers turn to other occupations. Like most trade unions, the teachers' federations have reacted to this redundancy problem by protecting seniority. The last one hired should be the first one fired. Seniority is now almost as important as salary. Is this good for the profession? Some would turf out the "dead wood" and replace them with new "super rookies." Others believe the "older teachers," those who kept the system going through the lean years in the 1960s and 1970s, must be protected.

It is a complex situation. The subject one teaches is as important as

Secondary School Transfer and Hiring Schedule

Monday	Tuesday	Wednesday	Thursday	Friday
Jan. 25 Regional seniority	26	27	28	29
Feb. 1 Decide headship vacancies	2	3	**4** Post headship vacancies	5
8	**9** Appoint heads	**10** Post regional seniority	11	12
15 Regional staff computed	**16** Staff allocation to schools	17	**18** Surplus to region staff listed	**19** Voluntary excess staff listed
22	23	24	25	**26** Heads voluntary resignations
March 1	2	3	4	5
8	**9** School organization submitted	**10** Excess list Leave list Vacancies list	11	**12** Regional lists Notify excess in writing
15	16	17	18	19
22	23	**24** LIKELY WINTER-BREAK HOLIDAYS	25	26
29 Organization confirmed Post vacancies	**30** Voluntary transfer applications	31	**1** Post assistant head vacancies	2

5 Voluntary transfer applications	**6** Up-date vacancies list	**7** Appoint assistant heads	**8** Post vacancies list	**9**
April 12 Voluntary transfer continues	**13** Update vacancies list	**14** Unplaced excess listed	**15** Post vacancies lists	**16**
19 Voluntary transfer stops	**20**	**21** Excess staff administratively transferred and placed	**22**	**23**
26 Excess not placed become surplus to region	**27**	**28**	**29** Post vacancies lists	**30** Voluntary transfer re-opens
May 3 External advertising for positions where no excess available	**4**	**5**	**6** Post vacancies lists	**7**
10 Voluntary transfers	**11** External advertising	**12**	**13** Post vacancies lists	**14**
17 Voluntary transfers	**18** External advertising	**19**	**20** Post vacancies lists	**21**
24 Voluntary transfers	**25** Terminate regional surplus	**26** External advertising	**27** Post vacancies lists	**28**
31 Voluntary transfers	**June 1** External advertising	**2**	**3** Post vacancies lists	**4**
7 Voluntary transfers	**8** External advertising	**9**	**10** Stop voluntary transfer	**11** Fill jobs by recall or external

seniority. Some school systems treat each school as a separate entity with no "systems bumping." For example, if enrolment goes down in history, a mathematics teacher is not cut, even though the mathematics teacher may have the lowest seniority. Each subject is looked at individually.

If the school system treats each school separately, one school may cut certain subject teachers while another is hiring. Wherever possible, simple transfers are made. Unfortunately, teachers must often teach combinations of subjects, and the combination needed at the second school may not fit the abilities of the teacher who was cut from the first. Some subjects are protected; some are even expanding in spite of cuts.

As jobs have become fewer and fewer during the past ten years, federations have been winning contracts with tighter and tighter tenure clauses. Consequently, school boards and the superintendents have become much more careful not to over-staff schools. There seems to be a policy of under-projecting enrolments, and thus under-hiring. With a good supply of teachers available, they can always pick up a few in the fall.

This situation causes problems for the students. Classes are overloaded in the first weeks of the fall while new teachers are sought, interviewed, and hired. Then classes are split and many students have a change of teacher. This new teacher may be rushed into the front line with very little orientation.

The foregoing calendar is a sample of the hiring procedures for a large school board. Note that it starts with enrolment projections in mid-winter and barely begins the external hiring until early June.

Consider the effect on the morale of the teachers hired into school systems in today's climate—especially those hired in late September and early October. They have the least seniority. Unless they are in the few large school systems that are growing, they are almost certain to be declared surplus and maybe redundant the next spring. They are rushed into the classroom virtually the day they are hired. They have no chance for advanced preparation of course materials. They have missed the school orientation programs. They often do not know how that school keeps attendance.

Just about the time they begin to feel they understand what they are doing, the administration starts to project enrolments and predict the need for staff for next year. In most systems some staff will, at this stage, be declared surplus. They receive letters (insisted on by their own federation's contract) to keep them informed of their tenuous position. These letters might read like the following:

Sample Letters

Feb. 23, 19___

Dear Mr. _____ :

In accordance with the collective agreement between the board and the _____ Federation, I am obliged to inform you that you may be declared surplus to the Board of Education as of August 31, 19___.

Enrolment data, resignations, leaves of absence and program requirements are reviewed regularly. A definite decision regarding your employment with the Board of Education for the 19___/___ school year will be forwarded to you in writing by May 31, 19___.

If you require any further information, please contact my office.

Sincerely,
Superintendent of Personnel

April 26, 19___

Dear Mrs. _____ :

In accordance with Article ___ of the collective agreement between the Board of Education and the _____ Federation, I am obliged to inform you that you will be declared surplus to region to the Board of Education as of Aug. 31, 19___.

A change in the above status may occur because of resignations, leaves of absence, and program requirements. These are reviewed regularly.

At the last regular board meeting in May, the surplus to region list becomes the recall list. Any teachers on the recall lists still under contract with the board will have their contracts terminated and will be notified by mail.

If you require any further information, please contact my office.

Sincerely,
Superintendent of Personnel.

May 26, 19___

Dear Ms. _____ :

It is with regret that I must inform you that the Board of Education, at its meeting held on May ___, 19___, terminated your teacher's contract effective August 31st, 19___.

This action was taken in accordance with the surplus provisions in Article ___, Section ___, of your current collective agreement.

Recall procedures are established as outlined in Article ___, Section ___, and will be ongoing.

If we can be of any assistance, please contact the office of the Superintendent of Personnel.

Yours truly,

Director of Education

After receiving such tidings, these teachers must still prepare good lessons and deliver them to their students. What of the morale among the rest of the staff? They worry when their turn will come, and feel sympathy for their colleagues going through this mental suffering.

This surplus-redundancy does other harm. All this is handled in a secondary school according to subject. Imagine the competition that must now exist for students. Those teachers who can keep the enrolment up in their subject are safe. How does one get students to take a subject? It becomes a popularity contest, with all the attending jealousies and accusations. The following chaos can also take place. A teacher has qualifications in two or more subjects. One of those subjects declines in enrolment; that teacher is lowest in seniority and so becomes surplus to that school. However, another subject in which the teacher has qualifications is holding up; perhaps there are staff there with lesser seniority than the teacher in question.

In many cases, most teachers declared surplus and even later declared redundant will find jobs eventually in that school system.

What advice can be given to new teachers?

— Have nerves of steel.

- "Get a foot in the door." Do not become discouraged in the spring. Most of the jobs will come up in the last part of June, in the summer, and in the early fall.
- Get as wide a range of qualifications as you can. Take all the courses the faculty will allow, and then take summer courses and night courses as fast as you can to get additional qualifications.
- In some provinces, school boards are required to offer a wide range of "special education." Secure those qualifications.
- Expect to be surplus in your school and possibly redundant to the system. Expect the letters. Find a shoulder to cry on.
- Keep an eye on other professions you could enter. But do not give up too soon.
- Keep informed of the contract and the job situation. Make use of your federation representative and the principal. Know the facts. Do not take your troubles out on the youngsters in your classroom or on your fellow staff members.
- Be willing to transfer to other schools in the system, especially to vocational schools. They seem to be expanding and have some problems obtaining and holding staff.
- Take heart from the future projections that say that birthrates are starting to go up; soon there will be more children and more jobs. Children are not going to become obsolete, and neither are teachers or schools.

Are there any solutions to the problems? Perhaps school boards and federations ought to abandon their adversarial roles. There must be ways to protect the senior staff without putting the younger staff through this misery. The transfer processes could be speeded up. Are all those lengthy interviews really necessary? Can enrolment projections be more realistic?

12 The Teacher and Computers in the School

12 The Teacher and Computers in the School

12.1 The Advent of the Computer

Computers have been around for a long time. Many industries, especially insurance companies, have been using them for the past three decades. School boards have been using them quite successfully since the mid-1960s, for purchasing, attendance, and report cards. Thus, the computer has affected the teacher but not the teaching, except business courses preparing students for data processing.

12.2 The Mini-Computer

Miniaturization has done wonders for calculators and computers. Machines that once filled a room and required carefully controlled climates are now in boxes one can carry in a suitcase. For the school, the first major breakthrough was the mini-computer. Contained in several boxes, each small enough and light enough to be carried by one person, this had the same capability as the large room-sized computers. They did not need temperature or humidity control, and cost as little as $20,000. Soon mini-computers began to appear in school classrooms. As recently as 1977, schools were still following this course; many of these mini-computers are still in use.

12.3 The Micro-Computer

Between 1978 and 1982, a revolution took over the computer industry. Miniaturization was accomplished in the extreme. The micro-computer performs functions the old room-sized computers could hardly attempt. The whole machine consists of several connected components (computer—t.v. screen—data storage unit—printer). All this can sit on a table top no larger than the average desk. The computer part itself costs from $500 to $2,000; with all the other components, it can be purchased for about $4,000. This price is coming down almost daily. Soon a computer or something comparable will be found in almost every home.

Schools no longer think of sharing a mini-computer; rather, in terms of class sets of micro-computers. Soon all schools will have them, for they can be operated by children of all ages. Every child will be affected, and every teacher is going to have to become involved. That last sentence sounds like those statements a decade ago about what television was going to do for education. Teachers were afraid that soon they would be replaced by t.v. screens. But about all t.v. did for most school classrooms was to provide a different way to show films, especially so since video tape recorders became common. Those who work so hard in the production of the many excellent educational t.v. programs on cable t.v. may disagree, but the impact has been far less evident than it was first predicted to be, or feared to be.

This will not be the case with computers. In the past two years alone, they have had a greater effect on education than t.v. managed in the past decade. The real computer age is just beginning in the classroom. Because of insufficient funds, there are only a few machines in each school. There are not yet enough machines on which teachers can learn and practise.

Once again, teachers are worried — "Will it take away my job?" Computers are here to stay. They will become so much smaller and better and cheaper that they will be as indispensable as pencils and paper.

12.4 The Teacher and the Computer

The teacher does not have to be a computer programmer, just a computer operator. This is no more difficult to learn than threading some of those early movie projectors. It just takes time to become familiar with the language of these machines.

In simplest terms: a computer takes on a job which can be broken down into a set of steps. These steps are numbered so the computer does them in sequence. It is the job of the programmer to break the job down into these steps and tell the computer (in its language) what is to be done.

What the teacher has to learn consists of two main, separate functions. First, the teacher will have to learn "scripting": to describe the steps of any teaching function to be put on the computer. This is not as easy as one might think. Second, the teacher must learn how to operate the machine. This consists for the most part in typing simple command words on a keyboard. Most commands are single words or very short phrases that can be typed two-finger style. The teacher who can "script" and the teacher who can "operate" will soon be using computers.

Teachers with mathematical, technical or business skills might want to become computer education teachers. The elementary courses in computers are not particularly technical and contain more historical and descriptive data than actual operation. There is a growing demand for this teaching skill. The increase in the number of students taking computer courses is phenomenal. One school went from two Introduction to Computer classes in 1981-82 to ten such classes in 1982-83. And they will move up to the more advanced grades, for more and more courses in computer science, data processing, bookkeeping by computer, and computer technology. In the above mentioned school of 1150 students, more than 400 are taking computer courses; many other students are using computers in their research or to help them study. At a time when teachers are worried about declining enrolments and loss of teaching jobs, teachers in computer education are increasing at a fantastic rate. The table below illustrates this growth in demand for computer education.

Data Processing, Computer Science and Computer Technology Courses

Pre-1970	1970-1980	1982	Future
	2 Grade 10 Introduction to Computers	7 Grade 10 and 3 Grade 12 Introduction to Computers	10 Grade 10 and 2 Grade 12 Introduction to Computers
1 Grade 11 Data; 1 Grade 11 Computer Science	2 Grade 11 Data; 1 Grade 11 Computer Science	2 Grade 11 Data; 1 Grade 11 Computer Science	4 Grade 11 Data; 2 Grade 11 Computer Science; 1 Grade 11 Computer Technology
1 Grade 12 Data	1 Grade 12 Data; 1 Grade 12 Computer Science	1 Grade 12 Data; 1 Grade 12 Computer Science	3 Grade 12 Data; 2 Grade 12 Computer Science; 1 Grade 12 Computer Technology
			1 Grade 13 Computers
60 Total Students	140 Total Students	400 Total Students	650 Total Students

Different departments can use computers in three ways:

The mathematics, business, and technical departments are very involved in the teaching of computers. They not only use computers on a day-to-day basis but also teach students how to use computers. They teach how the computers can affect everyday affairs. They teach how to program the computer, and how to use it to solve many different problems.

The art, languages, music, and science departments use computers in very specialized ways. In art, the computer is used for drawing and design. In languages, it is used for translation. With voice activated computers, it is now possible to carry on a "conversation" with the computer. The music department uses the computer to give visual and audial representation of music. (Composing music right on the computer with visual aids is one possibility.) In science, it is possible to simulate things that cannot easily be demonstrated by normal laboratory means (the inner workings of the atom, for example.)

The English, geography, history, library, home economics, physical education, guidance and office administrative departments use the computer to store and retrieve information. They also use word processors. With a device called a MODEM, the library not only stores data but also taps into other outside information services by connecting the school computer to them. A telephone receiver is placed in a cradle on the MODEM to receive electronic data over the telephone lines.

School offices have used the board's central computer for many years to do timetables and attendance reports. Soon all schools will be connected to the board computer over the telephone lines, to pull any data from the board computer back to the in-school computer. The guidance department also taps an almost limitless bank of data on behalf of the student to provide information on jobs and careers, about college and university courses.

The applications are limitless. Every teacher must get prepared. The introductory workshops offered on teacher professional development days are a good way to get started.

Once they have a basic understanding of the computer, the teachers can use the best resource for computer programming—the senior computer student. These students are often much more advanced in programming than the staff, and are well able to prepare the necessary "software" or programs.

With the help one gets from a few Saturday courses, the assistance of staff a bit more advanced in computers, and the programming expertise of senior students in the school one can really get started on most things that any teacher might want to do with computers.

12.5   The Computer in the School

It is best if a school system trains its own teacher programmers. The software can then be directed to the board's curriculum program and be tested and revised by its own teachers and students. In this way, the values content can reflect the orientation of the community. For instance, commercial games produced for educational purposes mirror the war and violence content of video-game arcades. Two programs developed recently by teachers reject the theme of violence — one deals with agriculture on land in the Niagara peninsula, the other relates to the production and refinement of oil in Western Canada. In the elementary schools, the students are also increasingly controlling their own learning through the computer. The Story Writer[2] illustrates this point: children choose and develop their own themes or stories, revising them with messages throughout from the computer.

Not everyone is completely in favour of computers in schools. Some teachers and parents say, "Kids will not learn basic arithmetic." In the forties, people cried out against slide rules; in the sixties and seventies, against calculators; now, against computers. However, sensible teachers have always taught the basics along with the machine. Just as the children are not worse mathematicians because of slide rules or calculators, they will not be worse because of computers.

Another argument against machines in schools is that "only the wealthy will be able to afford it." This is usually true for the first few years in the development of the machine. But, as prices quickly fall, schools can afford class sets, and many students can afford their own. Five years ago, few schools had more than one computer; today, most high schools have enough to keep a full class busy. There need not be one for each student. A lot of planning is needed to learn to program a computer. This can be done on the machine or from a print-out of the program. Thus, with a printer, two or three or even four students can manage with one machine. The same is true of disk drives. With a MUPPET, one can connect several computers to one printer or disk drive and thus save thousands of dollars.

Another argument looks at more personal effects on the teachers. With so many students choosing computer courses, fewer are taking other courses. Therefore, some teachers must shift classes; others may lose their jobs. Naturally, they are worried. It is the optional subjects that are mainly affected. Students must still take the compulsories like English and mathematics.

There is a great need for teachers in this field. Possibly traditional school organization will change in the future to allow computer departments. Such departments can co-ordinate courses in computer science, data processing, computer technology, and other courses of great value to students. There is good reason to suggest that at least one course in computers (Introduction to Computers) should be compulsory for all students.

Bibliography

Allport, F.H. *Theories of Perception and the Concept of Structure.* New York: Wiley, 1955.

Argyris, Chris. *Personality and Organizations.* New York: Harper and Row, 1957.

Bancroft, Glyn. "Report to Area 3 Superintendent, York Region Board of Education." Report of a workshop by Dr. Stephen Truch, Constellation Hotel, Toronto, February 3, 1982.

Barnes, L.B. "Organizational Change and Field Experiment Methods." In *Methods of Organizational Research.* Ed. V.H. Vroom. Pittsburg: University of Pittsburgh Press, 1967.

Barrett, I.C., *et al. The Legal Maze.* Toronto: OSSTF, 1980.

Bedal, C.L. *Guidance Services in Canadian Schools.* Toronto: Ministry of Education, Ontario, 1979.

Bennis, W.G. "Changing Organizations." In *The Planning of Change.* Ed. Bennis, W.G., K.D. Benne, and Robert Chinn. 2nd ed. New York: Holt, Rinehart and Winston, 1970.

Berger, P.L. *Invitation to Sociology.* Garden City, N.Y.: Anchor Books, 1963.

Berman, Paul, and M.W. McLaughlin. "Implementation of Educational Innovation." *Educational Forum,* 50, March 1976, 345-70.

Blau, P.M., and W.R. Scott. *Formal Organizations: A Comparative Approach.* San Francisco: Chandler, 1962.

Bouchard, Mary Alban. *The Courage to Create.* East Orange, N.J.: Global Education Associates, 1977.

Brief Look at Public Alternative Schools in Ontario. Toronto: Consortium of Public Alternative Schools, 1980.

Brown, A.F. "Reactions to Leadership." *Educational Administration Quarterly,* 3, No. 1 (1967), 62-73.

Brown, J.A.C. *The Social Psychology of Industry.* Harmondsworth, Middle-sex: Penguin, 1954.

Brown, L.B. *Building a Sustainable Society.* New York: Morton, 1981.

Burns, Tom, and G.M. Stalker. *The Management of Innovation.* London: Tavistock Publications, 1961.

Carlson, R.O. *Adoption of Educational Innovations.* Eugene, Oregon: CASEA, 1965.

Carver, F.D., and J.J. Sergiovanni. "Notes on the OCDQ." *Journal of Educational Administration,* 7 (1969), 78-81.

Catholic School. Rome: Sacred Congregation for Catholic Education, 1977.

Cedoline, A.J. *Job Burn-Out in Public Education.* New York: Teachers' College, Columbia University, 1982.

CERI. *Case Studies of Educational Innovation.* Paris: OECD, 1973.

Chinn, Robert, and K.D. Benne. "General Strategies for Effecting Changes in Human Systems." In *The Planning of Change.* Ed. Bennis, W.G., K.D. Benne, and Robert Chinn. 2nd ed. New York: Holt, Rinehart and Winston, 1970.

Clark, J.V. "A Healthy Organization." In *The Planning of Change.* Ed. Bennis, W.G., K.D. Benne, and Robert Chinn. 2nd ed. New York: Holt, Rinehart and Winston, 1970.

Coleman, James, Thomas Hoffer, and S. Kilgore. *High School Achievement: Public, Catholic and Private Schools Compared.* New York: Basic Books, 1982.

Conant, J.B. *The Child, the Parent and the State.* Cambridge, Mass.: Harvard University Press, 1959.

Corwin, Ronald. "Professional Persons in Public Organizations." *Educational Administration Quarterly,* 1, No. 3, Autumn 1965, 1-23.

Criscuolo, N.P. "Public Relations and the Classroom Teacher." *Education Digest,* 42, March 1977, 46-47.

Dale, Roger. "Phenomenological Perspectives and the Sociology of the School." *Education Review,* 25 No. 3 (1973), 1975-189.

Downie, B.M. *Collective Bargaining and Conflict Resolution in Education.* Kingston: Industrial Relations Centre, Queen's University, 1978.

Edmonds, E.L. "In Defence of the Private School." *Education Canada,* 21, No. 3, Fall 1981, 21-23.

Eichholz, Gerhard, and E.M. Rogers. "Resistance to the Adoption of Audio-Visual Aids by Elementary School Teachers: Contrasts and Similarities to Agricultural Innovation." In *Innovation in Education.* Ed. M.B. Miles. New York: Teachers' College, Columbia University, 1964.

Etzioni, Amitai. *Modern Organizations.* Englewood Cliffs, N.J.: Prentice-Hall, 1964.

Federation Update (OSSTF), 9, No. 19, Feb. 1, 1982, 1.

Fiedler, F.E. *A Theory of Leadership Effectiveness.* New York: McGraw-Hill, 1967.

Forehand, G.A. "Assessment of Innovative Behavior: Partial Criteria for the Assessment of Executive Performance." *Journal of Applied Psychology,* 47 (1963), 206-213.

Frederick, R.W. *Student Activities in American Education.* New York: Centre for Applied Research in Education, 1965.

Fullan, Michael. "Overview of the Innovative Process and the User." *Interchange,* 3, No. 2/3, 1972, 1-46.

Fullan, Michael. *The Meaning of Educational Change.* Toronto: OISE Press, 1982.

Gayfer, Margaret. *Open Doors: A Community School Handbook.* Toronto: Ministry of Education, Ontario, 1976.

Getzels, J.W., and E.G. Guba. "Social Behaviour and the Adminstrative Process." *School Review,* 65, Winter 1957, 423-41.

Gilbert, V.K. "Factors Affecting the Adoption of Innovations in a British Comprehensive School: A Comparison with Berman and McLaughlin's Model." *Planning and Changing,* 13, No. 3, Fall 1982, 181-192.

Gilbert, V.K., *et al. Perceptions of Educational Leadership.* Toronto: Ministry of Education, Ontario, 1977.

Gilbert, V.K., R.A. Martin, and A.T. Sheehan. *A Hard Act to Follow: Notes on Ontario School Law.* Toronto: Guidance Centre, Faculty of Education, University of Toronto, 1984.

Giles, T.E. *Educational Administration in Canada.* Calgary: Detselig Enterprises, 1978.

Gouldner, A.W. "Cosmopolitans and Locals, I." *Administrative Science Quarterly,* 2 (1957), 281-306.

————. "Cosmopolitans and Locals, II." *Adminstrative Science Quarterly,* 2 (1958), 444-479.

Greenfield, T.B. "Theory about Organization: A New Perspective and its Implications for Schools." In *Administering Education: International Challenge.* Ed. M.G. Hughes. London: Athlone Press, 1975.

Greiner, L.E. "Antecedents of Planned Organizational Change." *Journal of Applied Behavioral Science,* 3, No. 1, 1967, 51-85.

Griffiths, D.E. "Administrative Theory and Change in Organizations." In *Innovation in Education.* Ed. M.G. Miles. New York: Teachers' College, Columbia University, 1964.

Gross, Neal, *et al. Implementing Organizational Innovations.* New York: Harper and Row, 1971.

Gue, L.R. *An Introduction to Educational Administration in Canada.* Toronto: McGraw-Hill Ryerson, 1977.

Halpin, A.W. *Theory and Research in Administration.* New York: Macmillan, 1966.

Halpin, A.W., and D.B. Croft. *Organizational Climate of Schools.* Chicago: Midwest Administrative Centre, 1963.

Hanvey, Robert. *An Attainable Global Perspective.* New York: Global Perspectives in Education, 1979.

Havelock, R.G. *Planning for Innovation.* Ann Arbor, Michigan: Centre for Research on Utilization of Scientific Knowledge, 1969.

————. *A Guide to Innovation in Education.* Ann Arbor, Michigan: Institute for Social Research, University of Michigan, 1970.

Homans, G.C. *The Human Group.* New York: Harcourt Brace, 1950.

House, E.R. "The Micropolitics of Innovation: Nine Propositions." *Phi Delta Kappan,* 57, No. 5, January 1976, 337-340.

Hoyle, Eric. "Planned Organizational Change in Education." *Research in Education,* 3 (1970), 1-22.

————. *Planned Change in Schools.* Paper presented to BAAS, Swansea, Mimeographed, 1971a.

————. "Role of the Change Agent in Educational Innovations." In *Curriculum Organization and Design.* Ed. Jack Walton. London: Ward Lock, 1971b.

————. "Comment on T.B. Greenfield's Paper." *Educational Administration,* 5, No. 1, 1976, 4-6.

Husen, Torsten. *The School in Question.* Oxford: Oxford University Press, 1979.

Inner City/Private Education: A Study. Milwaukee: Catholic League for Civil Religious and Civil Rights, 1982.

Intermediate Separate Schools in Ontario. Toronto: Ontario Separate School Trustees' Association, 1974.

Jack Lam, Y.L., and S.L. Kong. "Effects of Collective Bargaining on Teacher-Board Relations." *Challenge,* 31, No. 1, 1981, 25-29.

Lipham, James. "Leadership and Administration." In *Behavioral Science and Educational Administration.* National Society for the Study of Education. 1964 Yearbook. Chicago: NSSE, 1965.

Lippitt, Ronald. "The Teacher as Innovator, Seeker and Sharer of New Practice." In *Perspectives on Educational Change.* Ed. R.I. Miller. New York: Appleton-Century-Crofts, 1967.

Litwak, Eugene, and H.J. Meyer. "Administrative Styles and Community Linkages of Public Schools." In *Schools in a Changing Society*. Ed. A.J. Reiss. New York: Free Press, 1965.

March, J.G., and H.A. Simon. *Organizations*. New York: Wiley 1958.

Maritain, Jacques. *Education at the Crossroads*. New Haven: Yale University Press, 1952.

Maslow, A.H. "A Theory of Human Motivations." *Psychological Review*. 50 (1950), 370-396.

Mayo, Elton. *The Social Problems of an Industrial Civilization*. Cambridge, Mass.: Graduate School of Business Administration, Harvard University, 1945.

Merleau-Ponty, Maurice. *The Phenomenology of Perception*. London: Routledge and Kegan Paul, 1962.

Merton, R.K. *Social Theory and Social Structure*. 2nd ed. Glencoe, Illinois: Free Press, 1957.

————. *Social Theory and Social Structure*. New York: Free Press, 1968.

Miles, M.B. "Educational Innovation: The Nature of the Problem." In *Innovation in Education*. Ed. M.B. Miles. New York: Teachers' College, Columbia University, 1964a.

————. "Innovation in Education: Some Generalizations." In *Innovation in Education*. New York: Teachers' College, Columbia University, 1964b.

————. "Planned Change and Organizational Health: Figure and Ground." In *Change Processes in the Public Schools*. Ed. R.O. Carlson, *et al.* Eugene, Oregon: CASEA, 1965.

Muller, Robert. *The Need for Global Education*. Philadelphia: Global Independence Centre, n.d.

Myers, D.A. *Teacher Power—Professionalization and Collective Bargaining*. Toronto: Heath, 1973.

Nobel, Trevor, and Bridget Pym. "Collegial Authority and the Receding Locus of Power." *British Journal of Sociology*, 21, No. 4, 1970, 431-445.

"New Women's Group Formed." *Federation Update* (OSSTF), 10, No. 8, Nov. 15, 1982, 6.

Newnham, W.T., and A.S. Nease. *The Professional Teacher in Ontario*. 3rd ed. Toronto: McGraw-Hill Ryerson, 1970.

Ontario Ministry of Education. *The Community and the School*. Toronto, n.d.

————. *Education Statistics*. Toronto, 1980.

Orlich, D.C., *et al.* "A Change Agent Strategy: Preliminary Report." *Elementary School Journal*, 72 (1972), 281-292.

————. "Change Agents and Instructional Innovation: Report 2." *Elementary School Journal*, 73 (1973), 390-398.

Owens, R.G. *Organizational Behavior in Schools.* Englewood Cliffs, N.J.: Prentice-Hall, 1970.

————. *Organizational Behavior in Education.* 2nd ed. Englewood Cliffs, N.J.: Prentice-Hall, 1981.

Parker, B. "Eight Basics for Good School P.R." *American School Board Journal,* 165, August 1978, 27-28.

Parsons, Talcott. *The Structure of Social Action.* Glencoe, Ill.: Free Press, 1949.

————. "The School Class as a Social System." *Harvard Educational Review,* 29, No. 4, 1959, 297-318.

Paton, J.M. "Crisis of Confidence in the Teaching Profession." *Teacher Education,* 8, Spring 1975, 56-66.

Porter, John. *The Vertical Mosaic.* Toronto: University of Toronto Press, 1965.

Presthus, R.V. *The Organizational Society.* New York: Random House, 1962.

Pyra, J.F. "Education and the Law of Defamation." *Canadian Journal of Education,* 7, No. 4, 1982, 35-56.

Roe, W.H., and T.L. Drake. *The Principalship.* 2nd ed. New York: Macmillan, 1980.

Roethlisberger, Frederick, and William Dickson. *Management and the Worker.* Cambridge, Mass.: Harvard University Press, 1939.

Rogers, E.M. *Diffusion of Innovations.* New York: Free Press, 1962.

Rogers, E.M., and E.F. Shoemaker. *Communication of Innovations.* New York: Free Press, 1971.

Report of the Royal Commission on Education in Ontario. Toronto: King's Printer, 1950.

Rose, A.M. *Human Behavior and Social Processes.* Boston: Houghton Mifflin, 1962.

Rosenthal, Robert, and Lenore Jacobson. *Pygmalion in the Classroom.* New York: Holt, Rinehart and Winston, 1968.

Sarason, J.B. *The Culture of the School and the Problem of Change.* Boston: Alyn and Bacon, 1971.

Saunders, R.E. *Financing Public Education in Ontario.* Toronto: OSSTF, 1970.

Selznick, Phillip. *TVA and the Grass Roots.* Berkeley, Calif.: University of California Press, 1949.

Sergiovanni, T.M., *et al. Educational Governance and Administration.* Englewood Cliffs, N.J.: Prentice-Hall, 1980.

Shane, Harold. "The Silicon Age and Education." *Phi Delta Kappan.* 63, No. 5, Jan. 1982, 303-308.

Sheehan, A.T. "Role Conflict and Value Divergence in Sister Administrators." Diss. University of Toronto, 1972.

Silverman, David. *The Theory of Organizations.* London: Heinemann, 1970.

Smith, L.M., and P.M. Keith. *Anatomy of Educational Innovation.* New York: Wiley, 1971.

Smith, V.H. "Options in Public Education: The Quiet Revolution." *Phi Delta Kappan,* 54, No. 7, March 1973, 434-7.

Stabler, Ernest. "Self-Government and the Teaching Profession." *Canadian Journal of Education,* 4, No. 2, 1979, 1-14.

Stewart, B.C. "The Cost of Education: Expenditure Ceilings, Weighting Factors." *Ontario Education,* 4, July-August 1972, 26-30.

Stewart, F.K. *The Canadian Education Associations 1957-1977.* Toronto: CEA, 1980.

Stogdill, R.M. "Personal Factors Associated with Leadership: A Survey of the Literature." *Journal of Psychology,* 25 (1948), 35-71.

————. *Manual for the Leader Behavior Description Questionnaire—Form 12.* Columbus: Ohio State University, Bureau of Business Research, 1963.

————. *Handbook of Leadership.* New York: Free Press, 1974.

Thomas, A.M. *Accidents Will Happen: An Enquiry into the Legal Liability of Teachers and School Boards.* Toronto: OISE, 1976.

Thomas, A.R. "Changing and Improving Educational Systems and Institutions." In *Administering Education: International Challenge.* Ed. M.G. Hughes. London: Athlone Press, 1975.

————. "The Organizational Climate of Schools." *International Review of Education,* 22, No. 4, 1976, 441-463.

Thompson, V.A. "Administrative Objectives for the Development of Administration." *Administrative Science Quarterly,* 9, No. 1, 1964, 91-108.

Tracy, Barbara. "Teacher Burnout." *Comment on Education,* 13, No. 1, October 1982, 12-16.

Truch, Stephen. *Teacher Burnout and What to Do about It.* Novato, California: Academic Therapy Publications, 1980.

Vienneau, David. "Teachers Suffer Highest Burnout Rate." *Toronto Star,* December 9, 1980.

We the Teachers of Ontario. Toronto: Ontario Teachers' Federation, 1980.

White, John, and Patricia White. "Comment on T.B. Greenfield's Paper." *Educational Administration,* 5, No. 1, 1976, 6-10.

Williams, J.S. *The Law of Defamation in Canada.* Toronto: Butterworths, 1976.

Wing, Robert. "Public Role in Teacher Self-Governance." *OPSMTF Newsletter*, June 11, 1982.

Woods, T.E. *The Administration of Educational Innovation.* Eugene, Oregon: Bureau of Educational Research, University of Oregon, 1967.